SOUL vs. EGO SMACKDOWN

How to say YES! to your Soul and
tell your Ego to ~~F* Off~~ Suck It.

TRACEE SIOUX

FORT COLLINS, COLORADO

Copyright © 2015 by Tracee Sioux

Cover design: Randy Beuth

All rights reserved. No part of this publication may be reproduced, distributed or transmitted in any form or by any means, including photocopying, recording, or other electronic or mechanical methods, without the prior written permission of the author, except in the case of brief quotations embodied in critical reviews and certain other noncommercial uses permitted by copyright law. For permission requests, write to the publisher at the address below.

Publishing House
Sioux Ink
737 S. Lemay Ave, Suite B4-156
Fort Collins, Colorado 80524
http://www.traceesioux.com
yes@traceesioux.com

Soul vs. Ego Smackdown: How to say YES! to your Soul and tell your Ego to Suck it. / Tracee Sioux -- 1st ed.

Paperback: ISBN: 978-0-9907762-8-4

Digital: ISBN : 978-0-9907762-7-7

DEDICATION

To Hoppy,

You are love itself.

My Soul has been blessed by Your Soul

in ways immeasurable.

#YESTHANKYOUMOREPLEASE!

THE PROMISE

Your Soul has a purpose,

It knows the fastest, easiest way to get there,

And it will never, ever steer you wrong.

CONTENTS

YOU HAVE A SOUL	7
GOD: THE WORD	9
I AM	15
BRING LIGHT	18
MICRO-PURPOSE	22
YOUR SOUL PURPOSE	24
RESISTANCE IS FUTILE	27
OUTSIDE VOICES	30
SOUL'S NEMESIS	32
SAFETY ≠ SAME	35
CHANGE = ENEMY	37
THE FORCE	39
THE SELF	42
THE SMACKDOWN	43
SOUL CONTRACT	46
SOUL MEDIATION	47
LOVE LETTER	49
BLAH BLAH BLAH	50
EGO'S TRASH TALK	52
BIG FAT BULLY	53
SECRETS OF SOUL	55
STAMP OF EGO	58
YES vs. NO	61
JK: GET REAL	62
YOUR PURPOSE IS ABOUT YOU!	63
THE PRESCRIPTION	69
TAPPING INTO FLOW	79
EXPERIENCING GOD	82

MEANT FOR YOU	85
NOT EVERYONE	88
DEAD PURPOSE	90
THE NEW PURPOSE	92
YES!	95
PASSION vs. PURPOSE	99
SEEK AGAIN	103
ONE SPARK	105
LET THERE BE LIGHT	108
IN-LIGHT-AND-MEANING	111
TANGIBLE SOUL PURPOSE	113
PROJECT LIBERATION	116
THE OUTCOME IS YOUR SOUL'S ENEMY	123
EGO PLAYS YOU	127
SLAVE MASTER	132
SOUL-FULL TIME	137
TIME JOY-GASM	139
PLEASURE DRENCHING	141
EASY vs. HARD	144
TIME TITHE	147
TRUE VALUES FIRST	150
ONE CHOICE	155
WHITE SPACE	160
SOUL'S MAGIC JUICE	160
INTENTIONAL SLEEPING	164
RESPECT THE MATTER	168
FREE WILL	172
SOULPRENEUR	174
LAW OF ATTRACTION	179
MONEY	181
THE BIG EXCUSE	181
SOULCONOMICS	185
THE GAP	191
WORK THE EGO	193
VISUALIZATION	195
SOULFUL SERENDIPITY	199

NOT 'TILL YOU'RE DEAD	203
THINGS ARE HAPPENING	206
FEELINGS EARNED	208
RED CARPETS	210

YOU HAVE A SOUL

You have a Soul.

Let's start with this basic premise. If you're hung up on this premise and can't get around even the idea that there is a part of you which is of a higher nature then either put this book down and go about your business with a different guiding paradigm or employ Suspension of Disbelief.

You're already quite good at Suspension of Disbelief because it's the cognitive skill that you use to buy into a science fiction movie with blue folks who say "I see you" and for you to believe that this is really the only profound knowledge they need to create utter peace and enlightenment. It's the same mental function that you use when reading a romance novel which is just too good to be true.

To enjoy that film or novel you choose to believe it for a short period of time. You make a choice to just go with it so that you can experience pleasure, satisfaction or learn something.

So do that with this book. Whether or not you're invested already in the idea that humans have Souls or you maybe don't understand what I mean by that, just for the duration of this book let's agree that there is one premise that everything this book is based on:

You have a Soul.

Just so you get as much pleasure and useful information from this book let's also agree that everything I'm about to tell you is at least possibly true. That it's not "fact" or "the truth," but that it's one credible way for you to think about the different voices in your head which are always telling you what to do.

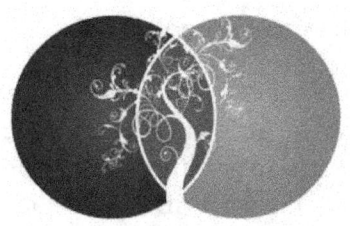

GOD: THE WORD

This is not a conversion book. This is not one of those books that end with me telling you to find Jesus. It's not a book promising to lead you to salvation. I will not ask you to confess your sins or embrace your unworthiness as a path to heaven.

This book won't encourage you to take up any particular spiritual practice, though I will encourage you to pick up a spiritual practice or two to aid you in Soul Whispering.

I have no allegiance to any particular faith, creed or religion.

But, I have faith.

And I will ask you to try things that will require a great deal of faith.

In your Soul.

Not in any particular deity identity or group that gathers in the name of one god or another.

This book is not a secular book.

The whole book is built around the idea that there is some force that is greater and more expansive and intelligent than any individual human is. And that we can interact with this force in a way that leads to more happiness and to more "getting what we want."

Most of the book will be me throwing down a challenge for you to have faith in that force.

You are part of that force. My intention with this book is to help you tap into that force so that you can be more *you* and to have faith that this *you* is a brilliant genius who is so critical to the Universe that you must do your work or we all lose.

Some people call this force God.

God
Jesus
Allah
Ganesh
Buddha
Mama Earth
The Higher Self
Spirit
The Universe
The Light
Collective Consciousness
Consciousness
Gaia

Aphrodite
Goddess
Energy

These are names people use for this force I'm speaking of. It's only human that ancient people attempted to personify God. It helped them make sense of this force. Relating God's relationship to humans as family (father and son, God's children) made God relatable, accessible and also provided the idea that there actually is a relationship between God and humans, which is more comforting, I think, than a belief that this force is arbitrary, random or doesn't feel one way or another about us.

We need someone to cry out to when we're on our knees in struggle and grief, we also need someone to shout to in gratitude and triumph.

So we have personified and anthropomorphized God as mythological gods and goddesses, animal totems, a man in a toga and beard sitting on a throne and even humans who have reached an elevated vibration of consciousness that is God-like.

However, God has become such a trigger word due to abuse, suppression of freedom and even violence, crimes against humanity and genocide that more and more people are moving from a personified God to a "consciousness" God in both understanding and language.

I use God and the Universe interchangeably. I believe in God. But, not God as a man in a robe and white beard sitting in judgement of us. I believe God is an ever-expanding consciousness of which we are all a part. God created us and the out of the same creation juice we create ourselves and our own little Universes.

Having a one-word simplification of the Universe's creation force is helpful for conversation.

No particular church or religion owns the word God or gets to define God. To even think that you know the infinite number of things there are to know about God is tremendously egoic.

So, what I'm saying is that I know many of you are triggered by the word God. It makes you tighten into a ball of angst and harden your shoulders to hold off the big "sell" that you're a sinner and you have to follow a prescribed set of rules or you're going to hell, oh and toss us some money on the way out the door cause "God said."

This is not that book.

But, I'm gonna use the word God. It's convenient and a widely acknowledged word that signifies the force I'm talking about. Most of the Western world can relate to the word in some capacity.

I'm not going to temper my use of the word God because somewhere someone was an asshole in the name of God.

Because they don't own God.

Trying to guard my language gives them way too much power over God.

I'm taking God back.

The Universe is another piece of the force that I will refer to. But, please, I'm going to trust you to substitute any word that makes you feel comfortable. I'll use a variety of words interchangeably.

I'm also going to quote the Bible now and again, because there's some useful wisdom in there. I might also quote Buddha or Hindu gods and goddesses and maybe even some Star Trek. We'll just see where this book takes us. There is wisdom everywhere we look and many cultures and religions have been seeking to put words to this force and so we will use the words of a diverse range of humanity and human history and perspectives and paradigms to seek our answers.

Jesus said, "Those who have ears, let him hear what the Spirit is saying ... "

Meaning, tap in to the wordlessness of this force while reading this book or any other. It's the meaning behind the words that are of interest. I'm using words to convey meaning and if you have ears to hear this particular message it will resonate with you. If you don't, that's okay, bless your Soul, put the book down and go on about your business in the world.

Okay, so now I'm going to write a book with this agreement between myself and you, my reader.

TRACEE SIOUX

You have a Soul.

You are a piece of God.

You're going to buy in for the duration of this book.

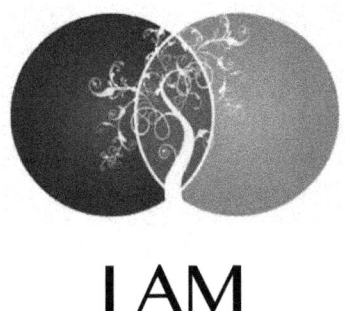

I AM

Your Soul is the part of you that is God

I AM who I am.

When asked by Moses, this is what God named himself.

I AM.

Hey, wait a minute.

I AM too.

And you AM too.

And Jesus said he was I AM too.

We all AM.

There's this big magnificent inconceivable enormous unnamable indescribably profound vast expansive genius knowing intelligence consciousness spirit called I AM.

And we am part of it.

Every culture, every tradition, every religion, race and science has pondered the same questions: who are we and what are we doing here?

God's answer?

SOUL vs. EGO SMACKDOWN

I AM.

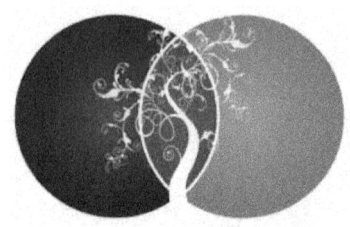

BRING LIGHT

It is human nature for us to ask the questions: Who am I and what am I doing here?

I take that to mean that somewhere deep within ourselves we inherently know there *is* an answer to the question. So we seek it.

It takes a level of faith to even believe that there is an answer to seek.

Who are we and what are we doing here?

Who am I and what am I doing here?

You can look at this on a macro-level and wonder why the human race exists and what is planet earth doing floating around the Universe and who or how did all of this come into being and for what reason or purpose does the whole shebang of life exist?

When you look to science for an answer you're greeted with theories of evolution and survival of the species and the big bang theory and string theory and on and on.

Still, behind every scientific question is a spiritual question that was asked long before science was even invented: Who are we and why are we here?

Physics, evolution, some say. Then, why does the species even care if it survives? Why do we have individual personalities? Why do we have different wants and needs and thoughts? Why do feelings even exist?

You can look to religion for an answer, greeted with an all-knowing God that must be appeased, who isn't all that keen on its own creation of humans and follow the mythology of various traditions and religions looking to be saved from the human condition by something bigger than themselves.

Behind all seeking is a very personal question: who am I and what am I supposed to be doing with my life?

Luckily, I have the answer for you in three simple steps that will make you unbelievably rich if you just believe! And it will make you thinner! And in the perfect bliss of a healthy dynamic relationship! So just keep on reading!!

Just kidding. Seriously these questions have been pondered for millennia and most likely we won't know "the answer," because the question is where the magic is anyway. Only the Ego believes that it is possible to even *know* the answer. But as we will find out through this book, the Ego is a nasty little liar.

I'm going to boil the macro-purpose down to God's first command found in Genesis:

BRING LIGHT.

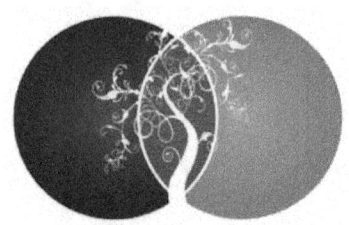

MICRO-PURPOSE

The macro-purpose is to Bring Light, but what each of us wants to know is, *what am I doing here, what am I supposed to be doing with my life? Do I even have a purpose and if so, how do I find out what it is and how do I make it happen?*

So that's what we're going to explore.

J.C. tells us, "Ask and it shall be given to you, seek and you shall find, knock and the door shall be opened to you." I believe this is a recipe for how things are made manifest into the world. Ask the question, get the answer. Seek your purpose, be rewarded with finding it. Knock on the door and get that contract or book deal or diploma you've always wanted.

We shall ask.

We shall seek.

We shall knock.

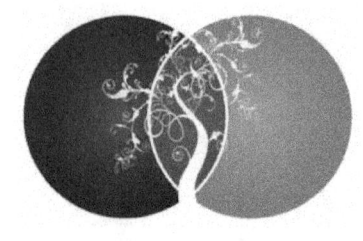

YOUR SOUL PURPOSE

Your Soul has a purpose.

You are an eternal spiritual being—a Soul—having a human experience.

There are many theories and beliefs about why your Soul came here or what purpose you're here to serve.

It's so heavy that you can get bogged down in the mystical aspects of life and never actually serve your purpose.

You don't really have to know the reason why you're supposed to do what you're supposed to do. You only have to do it.

When you are living your purpose you wake up in the morning ...

>with a reason to live.

with a drive to do something.

with a feeling of contentment.

with a reason to keep pushing through when things get hard or sticky or downright shitty.

If you aren't living your purpose it doesn't matter how pretty the picture is on the outside—great marriage, healthy, smart kids, nice house, cool car, great job—there's always going to be a nagging discontent that will never leave you be. You won't be able to put your finger on what it is or why.

You might even shame yourself for not being grateful enough for everything wonderful in your life.

Why can't I be happy? What is wrong with me? I have everything everyone wants and I'm still not happy? I should be more grateful!

This could go on for years, decades even.

You could live your whole life with a nagging feeling that you're not where you're supposed to be.

That's your Soul, darling.

That's the discontent of your Soul.

There's more, she whispers. So much more. Stop wasting time doing all of this busyness that is not about what you're here to do. We're not here forever, we have really important work to do. Let's get about our business and focus.

But, you're too busy to pay attention, you're too distracted by all the noise in your life, you're too scared to admit that you want something other than what you have or you are overtly turning your back on this inner calling.

Truly what you're hoping is that this irritating whispery voice will just go away and stop bothering you so you can live your life according to the "plan."

Because what this voice is telling you is down right terrifying.

It's scary.

It's not the plan.

It's going to upset the delicate balance of your life.

People might not approve.

Your spouse might be disappointed.

You don't have enough money.

You're clean out of time.

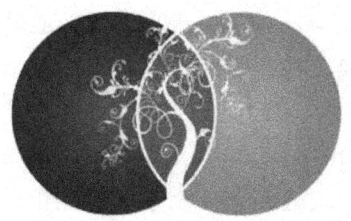

RESISTANCE IS FUTILE

That voice—your Soul—is never, ever going to shut up and leave you alone.

You can run from it.

You can hide.

You can tell it to fuck off and stop trying to ruin your life.

You can distract yourself.

You can stay in the swamp of busyness.

You can stick your tongue out at it and say *nanny nanny boo boo*.

You can confront it with spreadsheets.

You can try to reason with it.

You can demand that it justify itself with good reasons.

You can take pills or drink alcohol to dull the sound of it. You can even bliss it out with organic marijuana and pretend you're being enlightened by being zoned out.

You can pop antidepressants hoping that voice is some form of temporary insanity. (Seriously, take the antidepressants if you need them. I do.)

You can move, hoping for a geographical cure.

You can blame it on your spouse or your parents or your kids.

You can go from one job to another, chasing the latest fad for a dollar.

You can bind yourself to a religion that won't approve.

You can insist on knowing the outcome before you do it.

You can peter around with it, but insist on "perfection" before you produce.

You can hide in atheism and adamantly insist that you're just a ball of atoms.

You can shield yourself with cynicism and sarcasm.

But, it won't work.

Your Soul is eternal and it came here with something that it needs to do. And it's not ever going to give up on you or shut up about it.

SOUL vs. EGO SMACKDOWN

Your Soul's voice can be a sweet encouraging melody or it can be like nails on a chalkboard that drives you to insanity.

You decide which one it will be by whether you surrender to or resist to what it's asking of you.

The choice is really yours.

Nonetheless, your purpose is your purpose and you're stuck with it.

You can live it.

Or you can not.

Still, only one path leads to happiness and contentment.

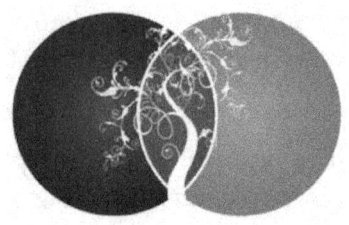

OUTSIDE VOICES

Of course we all have a litany of voices in our heads. I once did a psychological evaluation in college. The shrink asked me, "Do you hear voices?"

I knew the answer was supposed to be no.

But, yeah. I hear voices in my head all the time.

So do you.

It's inescapable. While I don't believe that hearing voices is a symptom of craziness I do know that allowing those voices to go unchecked can cause a certain level of insanity.

Just try to silence your mother's voice. I dare you.

This world is a very, very noisy place.

Parents, children, siblings, extended family, your boss, your coworkers, your teachers, your colleagues, culture, religion, media, marketing, politics, Dr. Phil, Oprah, Tony Robbins, Fox News, CNN, the Internet, Facebook,

SOUL vs. EGO SMACKDOWN

Twitter, other social media platforms, Netflix, movies, television, novels, self-help books, science, neighbors, the PTA, your mommy group, your friends, your best friend, your writers circle, the golf league, the bingo club, your bowling league, charity, school, education and standardized tests, business coaches and spiritual gurus all telling you what to do and who to be.

Everyone has an agenda for your life.

EVERYONE has an agenda for YOUR life.

Unless we're intentional and conscious about being in integrity with ourselves we will default to those outside voices and run ourselves ragged trying to meet everyone else's needs and people please ourselves into the grave.

As selfless as that sounds ... it's a death trap.

It will never, ever lead to happiness.

Because there are too many agendas, if you please your mom, your spouse might be disappointed. If you please your kids, your boss might be upset. If you please the church, your culture might take offense. If you follow one diet plan the next one will tell you that it will make you fat.

You. Cannot. Please. Others. As. Your. Purpose.

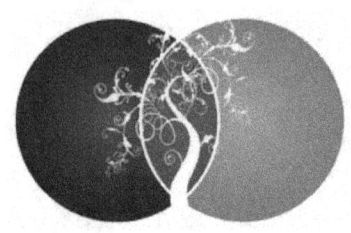

SOUL'S NEMESIS

There's another voice that is more insidious than other outside voices, though it often uses the other outside voices in collaboration with its agenda: the Ego.

What is the Ego?

The Ego is the part of you that tells you that you're not good enough, no one loves you, you're only meant for a shitty customer service retail job, you'll never get what you want and that you suck.

This voice often wins against the Soul's voice because it's louder and many of the other outside voices are echoing its sentiments.

You can't be a writer, no one makes money doing that, your Ego might parrot your mother.

Well, it must be true right? I mean two trusted sources—this voice in my head and my mom—are telling me this, so I must believe it.

The Ego is a tricky motha.

SOUL vs. EGO SMACKDOWN

It's brilliant at what it does.

But what does the Ego want? Why is it going to all this effort to sabotage you?

Safety.

The Ego is this primordial part of your brain leftover from cromagnum days. Its goal is to keep you alive. To keep you alive it uses fear.

Remember that movie *The Croods*? The father, Grug, wants to keep his family alive so he never lets them go outside of their nice, safe, dark cave except when they absolutely have to hunt and gather food. The family is primarily on board with this method of survival. It's a dangerous world out there and they really might get eaten by a beast.

The teenage daughter, Eep, of course, is dying to see what's out in the world and knows there has to be something more than this monotonous fearful existence. She wants meaning, connection with others, adventure, sunlight and fun.

Your Ego is Grug. It wants to keep you safe. It's a scary world out there and you need to stay in your nice, safe, dark cave unless you absolutely have to go out and hunt.

All of those other outside voices—parents, culture, media, PTA, boss—are the compliant family willing to stay in the cave and follow the orders of the patriarch in service to survival and safety.

TRACEE SIOUX

Eep, of course, is your Soul.

LIVE, she shouts! The world is amazing and it's worth the risk to LIVE.

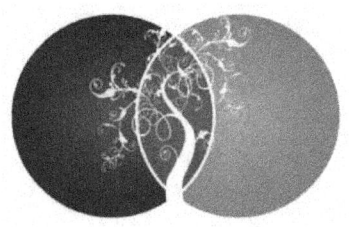

SAFETY ≠ SAME

The Ego confuses safety with same.

Wherever you are now, the Ego is happy to try to make you stay here.

This is where the phrase "the devil you know" comes from.

Your Ego would rather stay with the devil you know than risk the unknown. The unknown is the most terrifying thing that the Ego can possibly think of.

It does not want you to die.

In order to keep you safe the Ego will desperately try to keep you in the same place doing the same thing forever.

This is how people end up doing a job they loathe for 35 years.

The Ego loves Same.

Same Soul-sucking job.
Same terrible marriage.
Same addiction.
Same house.
Same friends.
Same school.
Same church.
Same political party.
Same. Same. Same.

The Ego's primary goal is to keep you in Same.

This is kind of why it's a load of crap to tell someone to *follow your feelings*, or *follow your bliss*.

Because:

When you make a Big Leap in favor of your Soul's purpose your feeling is FEAR.

When you stay in your Ego-sanctioned box your feeling is comfort and safety.

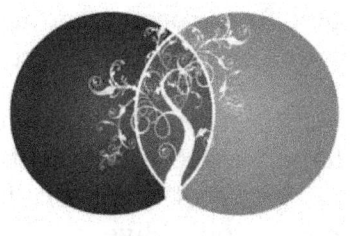

CHANGE = ENEMY

If the Ego loves Same, its enemy is Change.

The Soul's function is Change. Your Soul wants to do its thing in order to grow and expand in knowledge and experience.

Which means it doesn't have any interest in your working at the same job for 35 years, especially if you hate it.

It doesn't have a stake in you having the same social circles your whole life, because new people bring new situations and energy.

It doesn't much care if your marriage stops working and it's time to move on to expand its experience of love.

It doesn't look all that carefully at your bank statements, income or budget. It's an eternal being and it doesn't really believe in the confines of material matter. From its perspective the material earth realm is the illusion, the spirit realm is the real(i)tie.

The Soul came here for a purpose and it intends to live it regardless of your human external circumstances.

The Soul is also completely and utterly fearless. This is because it is eternal. There is no death for the Soul. There is simply a retiring of this particular human suit. Therefore keeping you alive isn't its primary motivation.

The dichotomy of the Ego and the Soul is the reason that it feels like a Big Leap when you stop in your tracks and abandon the plan and begin to follow your Soul.

If you feel like you're in conflict with yourself that's because you ARE. Your Ego wants one thing. Your Soul wants something completely different.

You: you are a Self that has free will and the right to choose which path you take.

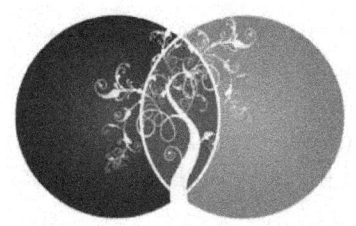

THE FORCE VS. THE DARK SIDE

Why are so many of our myths and stories about the battle between good versus evil.

Will you choose the Force or the Dark Side, Luke?

It's such a common theme because we are all faced with this exact internal conflict.

Soul. Ego. Soul. Ego.
Soul. Spouse. Soul. Spouse.
Soul. Others. Soul. Others.
Heart. Head. Heart. Head.
Desire. Reason. Desire. Reason.
Jesus. Satan. Jesus. Satan.
Heaven. Hell. Heaven. Hell.
Right. Wrong. Right. Wrong.
Light. Dark. Light. Dark.

These would be simple enough choices if they weren't so complex and confusing. Because rarely do situations and circumstances present themselves so tidily as Light or Dark, Right or Wrong. Though religions and political parties like to paint our choices as such.

Most of our choices are a little bit of both. The grey area just gets bigger and bigger as you age and are blessed with wisdom and maturity. The more you know the less things fall into clean categories such as the Force or the Dark Side.

Hell, we would all choose the Force if our choices were so clean cut, would we not? Even Hitler thought he was doing the "right thing" for Germany and the human race. And a whole lotta well-intentioned people agreed with him.

The issue is made even more confusing because this is a war between two essential parts of ourselves.

I mean, the Ego only wants to keep you safe and alive. And yes, it's kind of an asshole to scare you irrationally and to tell you that you're in terrible danger when you're really not.

Still, one can't go frolicking around the Earth realm pretending that our material human bodies don't have to abide by the laws of physics and that to break them could have dire consequences.

The Soul may not be too concerned with paying the bills, but the Ego knows that homelessness isn't the lifestyle you had in mind. The Soul may want to ski 100 miles an hour down a hill, but the Ego is going to insist on a helmet with paramedics standing by. The Soul wants to be in love, the Ego wonders if maybe a prenuptial agreement might be a pragmatic option.

So yes, the choice is yours.

Do you have the guts to say YES! to the Soul?

Or will you let the Ego terrify you into Same?

Wait, there are other factors at play here including your Self and the mind.

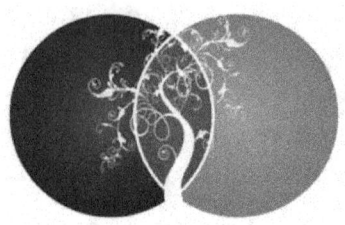

THE SELF

The Self is you, the personality, the human incarnation that houses the Soul, and your brain and the things that you think, your feelings, and the external influences that have combined to shape your psyche. The Self isn't all that eternal. It wants to live a happy life.

The Self is in control of free will.

Because you do have free will. You have the freedom to choose any path that you want on the planet. You have the freedom to turn away from the Ego and say YES! to the Soul. You have the freedom to walk away from your current allegiances and choose something more authentic to who you are.

But, remember the mind is kind of a liar too. And it's quite an effective tool for the Ego.

So, dear Soul Brothers and Sisters, you're going to have to go a little deeper.

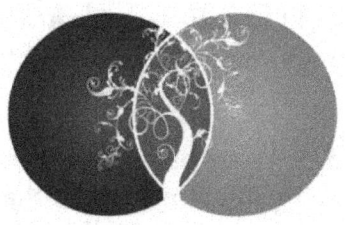

THE SMACKDOWN

With so many voices, how do you know which voice to listen to? How do you know which voice is your Soul and which is your Ego?

This is the number one question I am asked when I do this work with people as a spiritual business and life coach.

Say YES! to your Soul! I say.

But, how do I know which voice that is? they wonder.

I'm so glad you asked. I've developed a method of Soul Whispering which I call the *Soul vs, Ego Smackdown*. It's a writing meditation which will allow you to dive deeply into your Soul's consciousness. It allows you to see the contrast between that consciousness and your Ego.

Of course, this is best done either in person or at least on a recording so that I can walk you through the meditation. I'll invite you to take the ecourse that I created at my website, www.traceesioux.com

In the meantime, I'll do the best I can with the written word to help you with the exercise and trust you to get yourself into a meditative state.

To begin, grab a pen and paper. You can also get some candles and some meditation music if that will help you get into a meditative state. If you don't have meditation music you can go to www.clearmindradio.com it's a free 24 hour streaming meditation music channel.

For this exercise the first thing you need to do is read the Soul Contract aloud and then sign and date it. My original Year of YES! experiment was a commitment to say YES! to my Soul for a whole year. But, I find that people are less anxious, and thus more open to their Soul's voice, if they start with one short-duration commitment.

After the contract is signed I'm going to write out the meditation that I use to help people tap into their Soul's voice. You might read this through and then repeat it to yourself inside your head. You might read it aloud, you might do your own meditation practice to get yourself into a deeper state of consciousness.

It's very important to do several things:

   * Declare dominion over your entire being in every dimension and time including your physical body, energetic body, spiritual body and your mind.

   * Command all outside voices, including your Ego, to remain silent for the duration of this exercise.

* Invite the Soul and God to speak.

* Be open and allow anything the Soul or God want to give you. This could be words, sentences, visions, smells, scenes from books or movies, feelings ... anything.

* Don't demand to know the meaning of any of it yet. It might not make sense right this second and that's okay.

* Try to stay in the meditative state while you write. Write everything that comes to you, including what it feels like to have the outside voices silent and what it feels like when your Soul talks to you.

Once you're settled, turn the page and sign the contract.

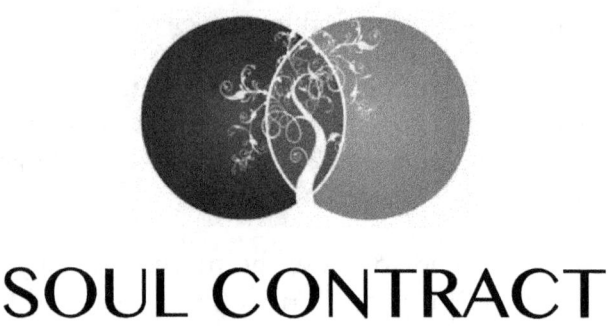

SOUL CONTRACT

Dear Soul,

I commit to hearing whatever you have to say about whatever issue you want to talk about for the duration of this exercise.

In return, my Soul commits to speaking loudly, clearly and persistently, so much so that I cannot mistake or ignore your message.

Love,

_____

Name, Date

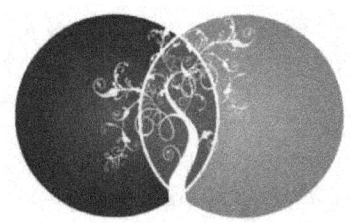

SOUL MEDIATION

Close your eyes and just take a few relaxing breaths deep into your abdomen. The breath is the force that keeps you alive, the breath keeps your Soul in your physical body. Take a moment to feel the breath move in and out with a consciousness and awareness that without this breath your body would cease to be, though your Soul would remain.

Feel your feet ground into the floor. Imagine roots growing out the bottoms of your feet deep into the center of the earth, holding you steady, tethering you to the Earth realm, even as you prepare to travel into the ether of spirit realms.

You have dominion over your entire being and your whole experience as a Soul and a human. You have dominion over your physical body, your mental body, your spiritual body and your energetic body. You have dominion over your energy and all aspects of you throughout all time, dimensions and realms of the Universe.

Declare that dominion now and command all outside voices to be silent for the duration of this exercise.

Your Ego must be silent, your mother's voice must be silent, Oprah's voice must be silent, your church, parents, culture, media, politics and all other outside voices must be silent.

We now invite your Soul and God to speak. Only your Soul and God are allowed to speak during this exercise.

The Soul is invited to share anything that it feels you need to know at this time. You may also ask direct questions. Be open to any word, phrase or sentence. Write down any feelings, thoughts or impressions. Record any knowings or inklings that come to you.

Do not question what comes to you or demand to know the meaning during this exercise. It's not your job to "figure it out," right now. Your only job is to listen and be open to what your Soul has to say.

You will not judge your Soul's gift or dismiss it. You will welcome all communication offered, knowing that there is meaning in it for you.

You may ask specific questions or simply ask the Soul what it wants to say.

Visions, images, smells, sounds, scenes from media, colors and all other impressions are all welcome.

Please begin to write and don't stop until your Soul is complete.

SOUL vs. EGO SMACKDOWN

LOVE LETTER

Date _____

Dear _____,

_____
_____
_____
_____
_____
_____
_____
_____
_____
_____
_____
_____
_____
_____
_____

Love,
Your Eternal Loving Soul

BLAH BLAH BLAH

Wow. Don't you just love that?

But, now that we've heard the Soul speak, we have another piece of ourselves to attend to.

The Ego.

Now, I know it's a very popular spiritual practice to dissolve the Ego. Some Buddhist monks spend their lifetimes sitting in meditation in an attempt to rid themselves of this pest. Hindus reach for an elimination of Ego into a sense of oneness. Christians try to forgive their Egos out of existence through confession and contrition.

All well and good. To be honest though, when I try to take down my Ego and dissolve it, it just appears to get stronger and more forceful about its own needs and desires.

Let me be bold and suggest that attempting to dissolve the Ego is a huge energy suck and will likely only lead to frustration and a sense of failure.

SOUL vs. EGO SMACKDOWN

So what do you do with it?

Well, first let's just hear what it has to say about what your Soul said in its love letter to you.

There's no special mediation for this part of the Smackdown because you're already well-acquainted with this voice and its recorded tapes. You've heard this song a million times. Once you get started you might not be able to stop. I don't want you to stop. Not until your Ego has had its entire say about the crazy pipe dreams your Soul just went on and on about.

When you go to the next page you're going to put your name on the top and write all of the objections and reasons that your Soul is reckless and bonkersville. Do not hold yourself back. Let it rip. Be honest about what's really true about your Ego's beliefs.

TRACEE SIOUX

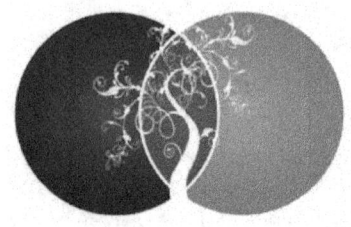

EGO'S TRASH TALK

Date _____

Dear _____,

_____
_____
_____
_____
_____
_____
_____
_____
_____
_____

Love,

The Outside Voices: Your Ego, your parents, your spouse, your children, church, culture, media & judgey neighbors.

BIG FAT BULLY

Ouch. Right?

What a big fat bully!

Don't worry, darling, you're not the only one.

When doing this exercise I've never had a person who did not look at that last letter with a bit of dismay. Some feel shocked and ashamed to have such horrible feelings about themselves.

But, don't worry, it's not a sign that you fundamentally feel unworthy or lack self-esteem. Even confident, capable, high-achieving people have an Ego that can get a tad nasty at times.

The difference is that they don't take it personally. They choose to believe that it's not really about them. They understand that the Ego is a liar. They understand that this is not the voice to be listening to and that this little undeveloped part of themselves is simply trying to keep them safe by making them too afraid or shamed or guilty to leave their little cave.

In other words, the only difference between people who live their Soul's purpose and those who don't is that one of these groups just does it anyway.

What I typically find when doing this exercise is that the Soul and the Ego have specific qualities and characteristics that you can point to to help you understand who is who.

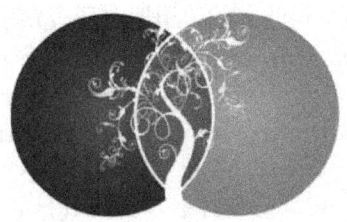

SECRETS OF SOUL

Souls are very loving. They are madly in love with you and believe that you are amazing and brilliant. They know exactly who you are and what you're capable of. They don't even entertain the part of you that is playing small. They hold you accountable.

A-count-able. They count your abilities and hold you to them.

Souls say sweet and kind things, maybe they have pet names for you and call you Love, Dear, Sweety or Baby. They lavish compliments on you and they know that you love positive reinforcement.

Souls are very comforting. They are not worried about making Big Leaps or changing directions or pursuing your purpose. They have a 360° perspective that allows them to see waaaaaaaayyyyyyy farther than you can see, so they don't think this next tiny little step is a big deal.

Souls might be frustrated with you. Don't misinterpret your Soul's voice as one that will never be angry or frustrated or impatient. Because your Soul has a purpose for incarnating as you, and if you're refusing to get on board and do what you're here to do then the Soul has every right to be jealous and frustrated.

She has been trying to tell you this for.e.ver.

Your Soul is not a new voice. You're at least vaguely acquainted with this voice. Even if you're surrounded by busyness and distraction you've caught this voice during a drive to pick the kids up from school having turned the radio off for a moment of peace and silence. Maybe you've heard it in the wee hours of the morning before your to-do list accosts your brain.

Your Soul is relaxed and doesn't rush. She doesn't really believe in time. It's just a human invention for convenience, so she's not racing toward goals very often. Her purpose might take a lifetime or more and so she's way more patient than you are.

Surges of creativity are a different story. Sometimes a Soul will see an opening and take it as fast as she can. She can be generating passion and fire that will help you jump into something you're supposed to be doing.

Your Soul isn't afraid and she doesn't use fear to torment you or emotionally blackmail you. Her game is love.

SOUL vs. EGO SMACKDOWN

Your Soul is the part of you that is God and so she often has an otherworldly quality to her communications.

When you're really listening and following your reward is a deep sense of peace and integrity.

The Soul wants you to be happy. She wants you to live a nice life with good love, wonderful health and meaningful work. She doesn't much care about specific numbers as long as you're able to make choices, give your gift and enjoy your time in this Earth experience.

Look at the handwriting. See the difference?

When you look at the two letters there is often a different handwriting. Some people have a very pronounced difference. The Soul is scripty and soft and sometimes it doodles and might draw a heart or rainbow or a puppy. The Ego often has hard pressing, underlines and angry bolding.

I had one client who went back and looked at old papers and journals. The goals that were all about money in specific numbers were in the Ego's block print:

I WANT TO MAKE A MILLION DOLLARS NOW!

Her checks written to charities were in the Soul's script:

Humane Society, $100.

You might go back and look at old journals and papers to see just who has been guiding and directing your life.

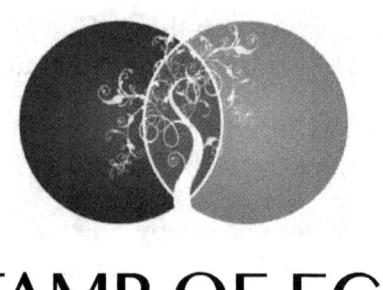

STAMP OF EGO

Your Ego is a bit of an asshole. That's right. He's a straight up dick, a world class bitch.

It would be so easy to write him off, except he has a point.

He has a lot of really good points actually.

His best weapons are reason, justification and rational thinking.

He loves spreadsheets and budgets, but he will rarely use them to tell you that you can afford to pursue your dream. No, he likes to use them to point out that you're really too damn broke to do anything of value.

The Ego is a huge fan of outside achievement goals. He wants to make "a million dollars" (Egos the world over are obsessed with this number) and will fixate on that number, insisting that anything less is utter failure. If you're preoccupied with the dollar amount of your income that's your Ego. Your Soul is motivated by something else entirely.

SOUL vs. EGO SMACKDOWN

Your Ego cares about big houses and status symbol cars and toys. Your Soul is much more down for an adventurous experience like a trip abroad that will be bonding for your family.

The Ego is not above calling you names: idiot, dummy, jerk, worthless, moron, bitch and asshole are some of its favorites. Sometimes I've seen Egos get downright cruel: whore, slut, good-for-nothing, failure and loser.

The Ego is convinced that no one loves you because you're downright unloveable, or at least it will tell you that to keep you in a shitty, destructive marriage rather than facing the wilderness alone.

The Ego's great weapon in the modern Western world is time. You're too busy to take on a Soul's purpose, you have a job and kids and a husband and a volunteer position.

WHAT DO YOU THINK YOU'RE DOING? YOU DON'T HAVE TIME FOR THAT AND YOU CERTAINLY CAN'T AFFORD IT!!

Its other standby is money. The richest country on earth and no one has any money. Cell phones, cars, houses, clothes, lattes, computers and expensive toys are probably in your life to some degree. But, for a Soul's purpose?

You're too broke and you'll never make money at it anyway.

The bottomline for the Ego is that you're just not good enough. You're not worthy of getting your big dream because you're just inherently flawed. This is where the whole Christian guilt sinner mythology comes from. You're inherently flawed because you sin and the original sin was the inadvertent act of being born. This is an irreconcilable unworthiness that you'll never break free of without constant repentance for ... being alive, wanting things and trying to be happy. You don't get to have those things because ... blah blah blah.

The Ego's handwriting is hard pressed to the paper, blocky and adamant, maybe some underlining and exclamation points punctuate its can'ts. This handwriting is often angry, rushing, and includes expletives like:

YOU'RE NEVER GOING TO MAKE IT, WHO THE FUCK DO YOU THINK YOU ARE?!?!?!?

Yep, the Ego is an asshole.

Who has a point about the budget.

Who has a point about your time.

Who really does understand how very imperfect and flawed you are.

Which is hard to ignore.

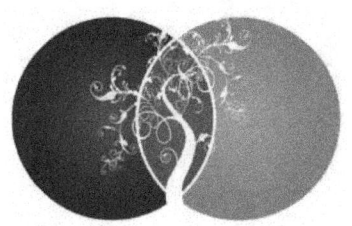

YES vs. NO

So, by now you obviously know that the secret is as simple as saying YES! to your Soul and saying no to your Ego. Easy Peasy.

So go do that.

The choice is yours.

What are you waiting for?

Change your life!

Live your purpose!

You're welcome.

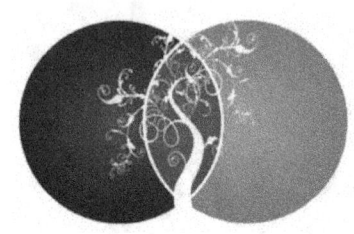

JK: GET REAL

Just kidding.

I'm really not going to leave you hanging like that. Because you're living a real earth life with real human concerns and if this were easy you'd already be doing it.

Plus, there are some really good questions left. Like what exactly is my Soul's purpose? Why do I even have one? What does that even mean? How do I go about changing the facts of my life so I can manifest it? Best of all: how, exactly, does my Soul think that I do have enough time or money for all of this purposing?

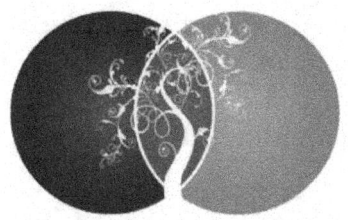

YOUR PURPOSE IS ABOUT YOU!

I want to start here before we get into what your Soul's purpose is. Because that will save you a lot of trouble as you are tempted to proudly, self-sacrificingly declare that your Soul's purpose is to help other people.

I do think that we're all here to help each other and a great many of us create communities around purposes. That's great.

Still, your Soul purpose has more to do with YOU than it does anyone else. After all, your Soul's purpose is yours. It does not belong to the others who might benefit from that purpose.

Please note: you don't get brownie points for having a Soul's purpose that is a charity or nonprofit. You don't get brownie points for being a teacher over a painter. You don't get to go to the head of the class if your Soul's purpose is more self-sacrificing. You don't get more good marks if your purpose leads to either poverty or success or fame. Your Soul's purpose isn't better than anyone else's, it's not more valuable or more altruistic or worthy of praise. It isn't less valuable or altruistic or worthy of praise either. All of that shit is your Ego's concern.

Your Soul's purpose is your Soul's purpose. That's all it has to be. Not good or bad, just yours. You get serious negative points if you forego your Soul's purpose in favor of something else because you think it makes you a "better person." Self-sacrifice is a sin against the Soul. You are *here* to experience this Self.

So, why does your Soul even need a purpose?

Well, why else would a Soul manifest into a human body with parents and a culture they are born into? Why else would a Soul experience the unpleasantness of pooping or aging, ailing bodies? Being human is dirty business fraught with risk. Earth is a high risk game in these extremely vulnerable human suits. Throw a human heart into the mix and the Soul learns what fragility really means.

There must be some reason for it. Some purpose to it. Some meaning.

Otherwise it's just too depressing to think of our random, meaningless lives going to work and taking care of our responsibilities, day in and day out. Eat. Sleep. Fuck. Pay bills. Yeah, you've figured out that the satisfaction of that kind of existence is pretty limited.

I believe we can know that we do have a Soul's purpose merely by the fact that we want one. The simple act of seeking more meaning and purpose in our lives and feeling that inner call toward something greater is evidence that we have a purpose for being here right now in this lifetime in this body in this culture in this incarnation in this time period.

If you dive into spirituality and theology you'll find a million philosophies about what we're here to do.

Some say we're here to learn things that we need to learn. For instance your Soul may need to learn more about forgiveness so you spend your life being treated in ways that need forgiving. But, that sounds fucking horrible, doesn't it? Just keep being betrayed or treated like dirt over and over and over until you can get really great at forgiveness. Same scenario if your purpose is to learn to stand up for yourself. If that was my purpose in this lifetime I'd probably just give up. It's too depressing. But, you might be here to learn more about love and kindness, which sounds like a lot more fun. You could be here to learn to make connections and build lasting relationships.

Some traditions say we're here to pay a debt or clear karma from other lifetimes. Don't you just love a paradigm that holds you responsible and makes you pay for shit you have no cognitive memory of?

Many say we're here as a quest to get back *there* (heaven —the big reward for living through this shitshow). The whole reason we're here is to make it back there, circle of life.

I grew up in a tradition, as a Mormon, where we were told that this earth experience is a "test," to see how we deal with our "trials and tribulations" and whether we can "choose the right" enough times that we progress to the next heavenly kingdom.

One day I was having lunch with a friend of mine. She didn't have a particularly religious background, nor was she particularly spiritual as an adult. We had just read Eckhart Tolle's *A New Earth* in our bookclub, which talks about being in the Now and staying in the present moment and how once humans figure out how to do this we create the experience of A New Earth—a version of heaven promised to us in the Bible. I was incredibly excited by this book.

I thought the purpose of life was to be happy, she said, a little bewildered at how complicated everyone was making it.

Happy?

Happy.

Wait, *happy*?

Could that be the whole purpose? For our Souls to become happy or try to make us—the Self—happy?

Could all of this sin and forgiveness and unworthiness and repentance and karmic debt and releasing all of our terrible limiting beliefs and ritual and meditation and religious history and all the wars over the Godness of your God versus my God be missing the whole fucking point?

Happy.

Could that be it?

I have to conclude that it's a possibility, a real contender. This was recently brought into a brighter light for me.

Last winter I got sick. Over and over and over it was one thing after another. A cancer scare and a minor surgery, leaky gut, terrible toothaches, root canals, flues and viruses, exhaustion and depression.

By the spring I knew what I most wanted out of life.

I want to feel good.

I wasn't concerned about my budget. I wasn't interested in my next professional goal. I wasn't fixating on the performance of my memoir *The Year of YES!*, I wasn't obsessing on when I was going to find my Soul mate or if I already had. I was ready to surrender all of that in service to this:

I want to feel good and be happy.

So darlings, maybe that's all you need to aim for. Be happy and feel good. I'm strongly considering putting HAPPY on my dream board and surrendering to whatever the Universe brings that will support that goal.

I want to make this declaration: *Whatever your Soul asks you to do will be in service to your own happiness.* It will not be in service to the happiness of others, except as a bi-product. Because what we know about happiness is that your happiness leaks out onto other people and blesses them whether you're just standing in their presence saying an encouraging word or you're bringing a homeless guy a sandwich.

Happy people make people happy.

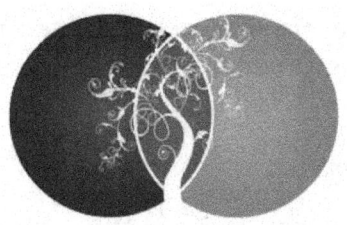

THE PRESCRIPTION

I know you're wishing that some authority figure will come into your life and say, *Jane, dear, you were put here to be a teacher of English of 7th grade students in Tampa, Florida.*

Then you would just have to obey and there would be no confounding questions or internal conflicts between the Soul and Ego.

Of course, many traditions have tried this method and the effects are ... complicated.

When a religion or culture prescribes every moment of your day from morning prayers to sundown prayers, Sabbaths and when you're allowed rest, what you can and can't or should and shouldn't do for a living, who you have to marry, how you should have children and raise them, some people feel extremely comforted by the structure and knowing exactly what the expectations are for success.

Still, others, like myself, feel a sudden need to revolt because we know one thing deep down in our bones, a knowing that courses like blood through our veins:

I am not meant for this.

And so you go running away from that thing that you know is not yours.

But to what do you run?

Do you know what thing is yours?

What should you be doing instead?

Many people run from something that they know is not their's and then they stall out. They have relief because they aren't in that paradigm anymore, but they don't stick with the discomfort or longing for long enough to start running toward the thing that is meant for them. They choose some secular rational path toward a house, security and relationship and figure that it's enough to have escaped.

But, something still calls to them.

A force that won't stay silent forever.

Their Soul.

YOUR Soul's purpose.

The big question is how do you find the thing that is meant for you? How do you know what your Soul's purpose really is?

SOUL vs. EGO SMACKDOWN

When I was 28, I was 32 weeks pregnant and waddling my way to work when the World Trade Center blew up in my face. Until that moment I had been living with purpose and I was really happy at that point in my life.

I was a writer. I had started in community newspapers and I was fortunate enough to be given an enormous amount of creative liberty to grow and experiment with my craft. I had positive mentors—all men of course in the newspaper industry—who wanted me to succeed and do well. I won first place awards for education reporting, a subject I felt passionate enough about that I might call it a Soul's purpose, and also for photography which captivated my Soul as well.

I moved into business travel writing for a trade journal in New York City. The work wasn't as fulfilling, but I was learning a lot and writing for a living and my basic thought was: who gets to be a travel writer in New York City? Me. I took free vacations and made a nice salary and had maternity leave all lined up.

I was newly married and we were optimistically planning our future and painting the baby's nursery and taking a birthing class on Thursdays.

After a pretty disastrous period that seemed to last from adolescence to my early 20s, everything was finally on track and we had our shit together. The future looked bright. I was doing what I was meant to do.

Write.

TRACEE SIOUX

On 9/11 the whole thing exploded in my face.

I took a photograph of the second plane hitting the second tower and my brain simply could not compute the information. I was standing next to a woman who was late for work, she would have been in that tower. I was close enough to see bodies fly out windows, but far enough away to not be in immediate danger.

I knew I had just witnessed the defining moment of our time. I knew that nothing would ever be the same. I knew it was terrorists, but couldn't comprehend an evil so vile that it would plan this act of heinous inhumanity. Like those towers everything in my world came crashing down. My body caved under the stress, developing edema and going into labor three weeks early. I suffered terrible depression and anxiety after the birth. It was like my body turned my terror response on and I couldn't figure out a way to turn it off. The peaked state of panic and anxiety I was in was such a terrible existence that I was miserable during almost all of my waking hours.

My marriage was still an infant itself and we were caving under the pressure. My husband had no idea how to support me through this terrible time and I really needed him to know. I needed him to tether me to the earth because I was no longer operating as a person who was living.

My maternal hormones kicked in with the ferocity of a mother lioness and I would not, could not, go back to work after my maternity leave. I couldn't leave my baby

SOUL vs. EGO SMACKDOWN

60 hours a week as I commuted back and forth from Brooklyn to Manhattan everyday. I begged my boss to let me work from home.

No.

The next-best idea was to freelance for my magazine from home, but just as that got revved up the travel industry collapsed with hotels and airlines closing left and right. There went the freelance budget. We were sinking fast and it was no favor to our marital bond.

I stopped writing. In truth, I was fucking mad at writing. I had sought out the profession intentionally, not only as my purpose, but for the assumed and imagined flexibility I would have by being able to work from home as a mom. Now that turned out to be a total lie. It wasn't that I couldn't. It was that my employer, and various employers afterward, wouldn't let me. Things are different now with telecommuting being a common practice but back then, let me tell you, there was a terrible resistance to mothering and working from home. A huge backlash.

It hurt. I felt betrayed by my boss. I felt betrayed by my craft. I felt betrayed by God.

I felt betrayed by my Soul.

I tried to go back to newspapers after that a few times, but it didn't fit me anymore. I would sit in city counsel meetings and think, I can't care about your pothole anymore. I just can't.

So I would crash and burn those jobs.

I stopped writing.

I stopped doing the thing that had carried me through childhood into my adult years. I stopped the thing that I knew was my purpose. I stopped the thing that I had committed my life to. I stopped the thing that might save me if I could only write it out and process this big huge trauma that was fucking my life up.

I spiraled into a deep, dark hole of depression.

I had nothing to wake up for everyday. Because the truth was I love being a mother and I loved my child, but I was also a very traumatized person who had just lost her place in the world and mothering wasn't enough of a purpose to wake me from a slumber to greet the day with excitement. It was a lot of work and I didn't have any energy to speak of.

If you want to know all the gory details you can read my memoir, *The Year of YES!*, but here let me say that eventually, after about five years I found myself sitting on my porch.

My life was a mess. I was smoking a cigarette, wearing a heart monitor because I had let my health go to hell, getting fat, drinking beer, eating Cheetos, never exercising and smoking was not making me happy, healthy or pretty.

My four-year-old daughter was standing at the screen door crying because the stupid preschool had told her that smoking kills people and she didn't want me to die. The baby was crying in his crib. I loathed living in Texas where we had moved with a mistaken misguided belief that we would find support there among family members.

This is my life, I thought.

This sarcastic statement suddenly struck me as profound.

This is my life.

MY life.

I had been living for the last four years with the question, What if I die?

What then is the point of making any effort?

What's the point of making plans or choices that lead somewhere if the entire world can blow up in your face at any moment?

Suddenly, I asked another question. A series of better questions.

What if I live?

What if I live? What is it going to take to make me want to wake up every morning? What kind of purpose or meaning can I find that will make being alive worth the pain and struggle and heartache of living?

Talk about a profound paradigm shift. On that porch I decided I would have to rebuild my life. I had been waiting for the next attack, the next explosion for five years and it evidently wasn't going to come. So I had to face the very painful idea that maybe I might live and if I don't change my ways I'm just going to be fat, depressed, unhappy and gross.

At the time, my daughter was in those precious little preschool years when they are so impressionable and I had been seeing the messaging of media and culture tell her who she was as a girl. I didn't care for the messaging.

Advocating for girls, empowering parents to raise powerful daughters would be my purpose. That is the thing, the cause, that would get me out of bed every morning.

So what did I do?

I started writing, obviously.

I started an advocacy blog called *The Girl Revolution*. That blog—that movement— carried me out of depression into the life of a living person. A person with purpose and meaning.

I wrote 1,000+ posts on topics ranging from self-esteem and self-worth, to eating disorders, sex abuse, domestic violence, employment law, politics, the glass ceiling, gender constructs and stereotypes. I took down the Disney Princesses and was featured in an article about early puberty in *New York Times Magazine*. I gathered a following and led a tribe.

That would be my purpose for seven years.

It woke me up in the morning, it gave me ambition, it never lost its shiny glow of attraction, it kept me constantly fascinated and it made me feel like I was doing something of value for the world.

My Soul's purpose saved me.

Back to the question, how do you know when it's your Soul's purpose?

When:

TRACEE SIOUX

Not doing it
might kill you.

Doing it
might save you.

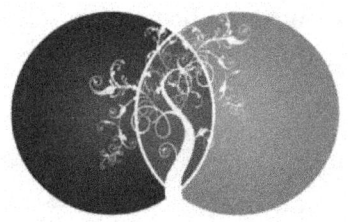

TAPPING INTO FLOW

If you can reach flow doing it, it's probably at least a part of your Soul's purpose.

There's this phenomenon that scientists, psychologists and the spirituals are researching these days called Flow.

Flow is a state of being where you're completely engaged, yet completely at peace. You lose time because you are lost in what you are doing. You love being in flow so much that you want to get back to it as much as possible, so you end up pursuing the activities that take you back to that place over and over again.

Funny thing, not everyone reaches flow the same way. I know a World Cup speed skier and he loves skiing because he drops into flow when he does it. The activity is challenging enough to keep him engaged, trying not to die, but he's also dropped into a more surreal state of consciousness. I went skiing with him and was so terrified that I might break my neck that I was nowhere near the Land o' Flow.

However, when I write, edit or play with words in any way I can reach a state of flow that is ecstatic within minutes of beginning. I can maintain it for hours and hours, days at a time. I can even reach the flow state when writing about engineering, processed chicken or pipe fittings.

People get into flow based on a few criteria. First there's a basic interest that makes you attempt a task to begin with. Numbers might fascinate you so you take an economics class and realize that you love analysis. Readers might be so observant of the holy work of writing that they pick up a pen and try their own hand at it. Some might be drawn to put their hands in the dirt to make mud pies as children to find that they feel most alive when there is earth underneath their nails.

Did you hear the word *alive* in that last example?

Whatever your Soul's purpose is, it will make you feel more alive. That is also one of the symptoms of a flow state. When you are in the flow or "going with the flow" you feel very alive.

People often feel flow doing their favorite sport—probably evolution's brilliant work to make sure we stay active, fit and healthy—it makes rock climbing, kickboxing, yoga, cycling or tennis so dang fun that we want to keep doing it. Genius!

The people who are really invested in their own happiness tend to figure out what makes them fall into a state of flow and then choose a related profession so they can spend as much time as possible there while they earn their living.

As a spiritual business coach I'm a huge fan of making sure that your Soul's purpose can earn your bread.

I will live by my pen, I have often (mis)quote Jane Austin to myself whenever I consider giving up the craft of writing professionally.

Do you know what I really think flow is? It's a state of being where we are literally touching God. We're tapped into our Soul-Selves and we're channeling the geniuses of creativity and the angels of inspiration. Our physical bodies become mere vessels as our chakras open and God Consciousness Spirit Energy flows through us, feeding us the waters of knowing and love that will finally quench our thirst.

It feels so good that it can make you weep.

TRACEE SIOUX

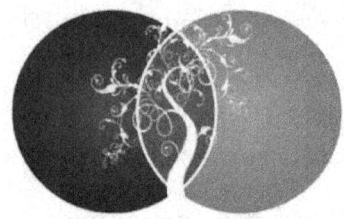

EXPERIENCING GOD

It feels so good to watch others do it too. We love to witness God.

This is why watching live music is so exciting and thrilling. A few summers ago I went to a Colorado music festival, *Arise*. I was excited to interview my friend Katie Gray of Sea Stars for *Year of YES! Radio*. I stayed to watch her partner Kurt Baumann play with his band *Kan'Nal*.

I saw God. I was transfixed and my Soul was jumping up in joy, arms over my head, *God! God!* in ecstatic recognition of that thing, the creation force. God Flow came in the face of the drummer, a middle-aged Indian woman with gigantic breasts who pounded those sticks with such abandon and joy that I, and everyone who ever witnessed her do her art, knew that this was her Soul's purpose. You could see the Universe's creative muses channel right through her into the crowd as the thumping of God's heart.

We are witnessing the act of creation when we see people perform or do art or do whatever it is they are called to do.

God is the creation force of the Universe. When we witness creation we witness God. When we participate in the act of creation we ARE God.

Please note that I do not believe that the God-drummer was called to pursue a life and career in music for my benefit. That joy is authentically hers. It was meant for *her*.

She was called to a life of music—a temptation as a younger self to pick up sticks and beat them against something, to stomp the rhythm and ring the bell and clang the tambourine—for her very own pleasure and joy.

My ecstatic pleasure at witnessing her was not due to her skill and technique, though undoubtedly she took her craft seriously and was highly skilled, my pleasure came from witnessing how God came through her, to witness her experiencing God.

See how that works?

You might not look at a list of professions and say, I want to do God's work and experience holiness, so I will become a drummer of a rock band.

Because who does that?

TRACEE SIOUX

The person who is drawn to the sticks, picks them up and finds flow, that's who. That person knows that this was meant for them.

SOUL vs. EGO SMACKDOWN

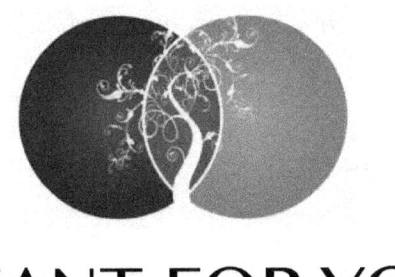

MEANT FOR YOU

You want what you want because it is meant for you. I don't want to get all simplistic on you, but it is pretty simple.

If it wasn't yours you wouldn't want it with this kind of thirst and hunger. Do you think that you are just randomly laying in bed at night fantasizing about creating the perfect pair of cycling shorts?

Everyone in the world is doing that right before they nod off, aren't they? Um. No. In fact, I've never, ever had even the fleetingest of thoughts about how to make better cycling shorts. I don't cycle. I don't make clothes.

I've been coaching people on how to figure out their Soul's purpose and then turn it into a profitable business for a few years now. Before that I interviewed hundreds of entrepreneurs and business leaders as a business journalist.

It always strikes me as odd that so many people believe that they can't have what they really want.

I want to make a line of cycling apparel, one of my clients finally got up the courage to tell me. This burning desire within her was something she just didn't tell people. She could barely admit it to herself. Yet, she spent countless hours fantasizing about what the clothes would look and feel like. Because it is meant for her.

Of course she's not allowed to manifest this creation because—no time, no money and she's not good enough —different Ego, same lie.

For some, the more you want it the more out of reach it feels.

Which is interesting.

Because why on earth do you think that you want this thing that is shouting your name and begging you to make it manifest?

Do you think this creation that is begging to be born, this piece of God-stuff that is floating around harassing you day in and day out, got the wrong address?

Yes. Many people do believe that.

I'm not capable of doing this, many people think. I'm not good enough. I need another qualification or certification or class. I need a big pile of money to make something like this happen. I need way more power and influence. I can't have this. It must not be mine because ....

I'm me.

SOUL vs. EGO SMACKDOWN

Haahaahaaahaaahaaa.

Yes, well, everyone is someone.

And guess who you are?

I AM.

I AM can do anything it damn well wants because I AM is I AM.

So there.

NOT EVERYONE

Listen to me say this: you want what you want because it is meant for you.

For YOU.

Many people fall into the trap of thinking that because you want something so fiercely that everyone must want this thing so this tantalizing possibility must be either way too competitive or hard to achieve or that they have to sell their Soul to get it.

This is madness. Madness I say!

Not everyone wants to own a landscaping company.

Not everyone wants to write novels.

Not everyone wants to be famous.

Not everyone wants to be married.

Not everyone wants to have children.

Not everyone wants what you want.

In fact, were you to look cumulatively at the world population and count how many people share your exact vision for your life you would probably be in competition with zero people.

Sure there are many authors, but not all authors want to write the same things and tell the same stories.

There are many actors, but some want to do comedy and others want to do drama and still others want to try their hand at porn. Pun intended.

There might be some authors who want to do what you do, but they won't be able to use the same language or voice that you do, because their perspective and their life experience is a completely different one. So they can write a love story, but they will have something different than you to say.

Your Soul doesn't care if someone else is writing about World War II. If your Soul wants to write about WWII, then just let it.

Your Soul doesn't care that seven great accountants are applying for the same job or that there is another dress shop two doors down or that there are already ten breweries in this town. Your Soul wants what it wants. What others are doing is really of little concern to your Soul.

Let me just point this other little bit of truth out:

People can want *and get* the same thing.

TRACEE SIOUX

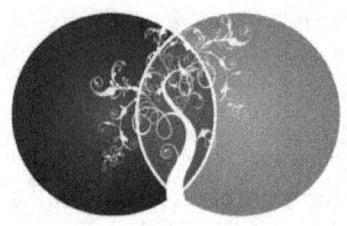

DEAD PURPOSE

So I wrote *The Girl Revolution*, and got some media attention and made a name for myself among like-minded thinkers and influenced millions of people with my Soul purpose project.

Then this crazy thing happened. I was about to take the national stage in the media with this area of advocacy that I had devoted my life to, and done so much work and research on ... and I backed away.

I backed away.

See, I was all about doing the work, but when it came to the national media wanting to use my daughter as the poster child for early puberty, I tip-toed across the line and then ran back for cover.

Was it Ego that got scared of coming out of its cave? Probably.

Was it protective mama that realized her daughter was about to go to middle school and it was time to stop talking about her in public? That too.

SOUL vs. EGO SMACKDOWN

Did Ego and Mama have a point? Absolutely.

After that I slowly, and painfully, realized that this purpose wasn't mine any more. I had said everything my Soul felt compelled to say after seven years and 1,000+ blog posts and a book. I had gotten bored of talking about it.

When your purpose is not your purpose anymore it feels like when you're pregnant and the whole process of pregnancy and birth is beyond fascinating. Then you are just so interested in breastfeeding and sleep training and getting that kid potty trained.

Then as your kids grow, it stops being so fascinating and you'd rather go to the OB/GYN for a pelvic exam than sit through one more birth story or argue about the pros and cons of breastfeeding over formula.

The purpose has been explored and experienced. Now it's time for a new one.

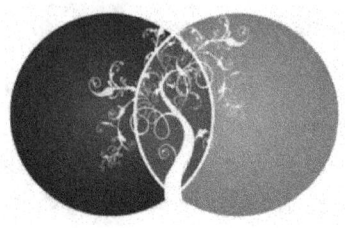

THE NEW PURPOSE

When you lose a Soul's purpose there's a gap period in which you don't really have one. It's disconcerting and uncomfortable. You realize how valuable a Soul's purpose is and the part it plays in your happiness and productivity when it's gone. You wake up and wander around aimlessly, sure that you're supposed to be doing something but not being able to name it or take action on it.

After *The Girl Revolution* ended for me (the posts are still up helping parents work through those issues, though I no longer write new content on the subject) I started looking for a Soul's purpose.

Of course, I knew my new purpose would be coaching and teaching people Law of Attraction because that is one of the methods and practices that saved me after my terrible 9/11 crash.

After I had my Soul purpose porch epiphany I saw *The Secret*. I came to the realization that this traumatic event had resulted in the belief that I have no control over my life. This event was completely uncontrollable by me and so was everything else. I had worked hard to build one kind of life and it had exploded in my face, through no act of my own.

Through Law of Attraction I began to exert control over my fate, my experience and my direction by getting very intentional about where I wanted to go, who I wanted to be and how I wanted to live. Law of Attraction saved me.

By golly, I'm really good at manifesting what I want through Law of Attraction. It is a consuming passion for me and something that I never stop talking or thinking about.

That's another sign that you're on the right track. You never get bored with the topic. You can entertain yourself for hours and hours, days, months, years talking about the thing that your Soul cares about. You can always take it deeper and talking about it or doing it always revives your energy in some way.

So I changed the title of my Facebook page from *The Girl Revolution* to *Tracee Sioux, Law of Attraction Coach*.

Here's a tip from a business coach: don't do that.

Don't rebrand yourself immediately after you think you've found the next Soul purpose. Because yes, you're on the right track, following the awesome clues and this feels so right that you can't believe that it could get better.

But, it can.

It does.

Changing your Facebook page is a once in a lifetime privilege and it's like a marriage because the only way out of the commitment is to start all over again.

I began to realize another quality of Soul purposes: your Soul came here for a purpose and that purpose isn't even about that one project or that one thing.

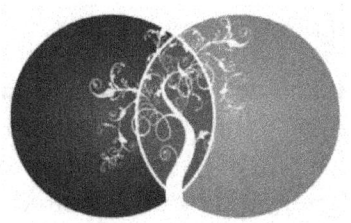

YES!

I didn't stick with "Law of Attraction Coach" in my branding, but I did pursue coaching.

I did this experiment in 2013 where from January 1 to December 31 I vowed to say YES! to everything my Soul told me to do. For the whole year. Without demanding to know the outcome. Without a good reason.

Just YES! to my Soul. Which meant NO to a lot of other people's agendas for my life.

It was an amazing experience. I learned so much about my Soul that year. I healed forty years of psychic garbage; it was a wild ride. I chronicled that life-changing journey in my personal diary.

The year after, 2014, my purpose became about publishing my raw and very personal diary/memoir as The Year of YES!: What if you said YES! to everything you told me to do for one year?

I HAD to publish that book.

My Soul insisted on it.

It was terrifying and cost me dearly in Ego-death to do it. It was an all-consuming flame. I hired a big, slightly scary New York City editor and had professional artwork and photography done, I hired designers and marketers.

This book was my Soul's purpose.

I knew it.

Finally on October 20, 2014 it came out on Kindle. Then we did a big publicity push to drive it to best seller status on Kindle and get reviews. Then I launched a group coaching program.

I was a Productivity Goddess on a Creative Bender. Driven by an otherworldly passion. A sense of Soul purpose so strong that others would just gawk at me in awe and disbelief. Well, okay, maybe that's a tad bit exaggerated.

I was literally having labor pains as that book was being born. I was physically pushing and having contractions in my vagina (that's what literal means folks). Sorry dudes, the mind-body-spirit connection is a real thing. I remember thinking, I have to get this book out now or my uterus is going to fall out with all this pushing and laboring. (Yes, after the book came out the laboring and pushing stopped.)

Finally it was January 2015 and I had done it.

The book was published.

I was proud of it.

I had manifested my Soul's purpose!

Now what?

If that was my Soul's purpose what was I going to do with the rest of my life? I was only forty.

The whole year felt just like the postpartum depression I had experienced after the birth of my first baby post 9/11.

Postpartum depression.

It was such a big piece of my Soul's purpose and my Soul had expended an enormous amount of energy to make it happen. Now my Soul needed to rest.

But, I like a good productivity high and rest feels so sinfully lazy and unproductive that I fought it.

I got sick and every time I started to rev back up into my normal push and go routine my body would lay me flat and enforce rest again.

I would start to feel better, head back to kickboxing where I would push too hard and then spend the next two days in bed. I recovered from a surgery only to get leaky gut. I'd had a root canal only to have a minuscule bite mismatch that kept me eating liquid foods and resting for 10 days while waiting for an appointment with a specialist.

Soul purpose postpartum. It's a real thing. Watch out for it.

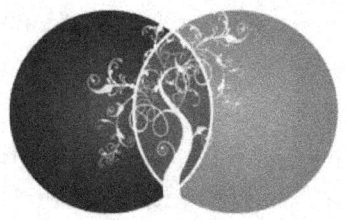

PASSION vs. PURPOSE

Find your passion and pursue it, self-help harpies tell you. It's okay advice if you're going full tilt on a purpose-driven project like a book.

However, passion is a dangerous mistress to court over a lifetime.

Passion burns too hot. It takes too much energy to maintain.

Passion can lead to burn out.

Which is what happened after I published my book: I burned out. I burned extremely hot for about six months and then came the big bang birth and the postpartum aftermath.

Ever wonder why so many brilliant artists and intellectual geniuses flame out on addiction, drugs, alcohol, partying and end up dead at a young age?

Passion.

Passion is great when you're motivated to finish a project. Passion is useful when you entertain it for short bursts of time.

However, passion cannot be sustained. It's too hot, too intense and requires too much mental, physical and spiritual energy. Passion can wreak havoc on your nervous system.

Purpose on the other hand is a nice steady moderate burn that you can maintain for a lifetime. Having a Soul purpose rather than a Soul passion is where you want to keep focused. Use bursts of passion when your Soul's purpose is served by it to get a project finished, but use it sparingly enough that you don't get addicted.

People fall prey to passion because they get addicted to the adrenaline rush. It's a high. It's a surge of feel-good hormones that can make you feel invincible. I'm tapping into flow and purpose and a side of passion right now as I write this book free-flow style and I'm feeling all tapped into a high vibration and soaking in God's inspiration juice and it feels *good*.

But it's not sustainable for more than its allotted time. I came to a Northern Colorado Writers retreat to write this book and to make space for a big push of passion to serve my Soul's purpose.

However, one cannot rely on passion to sustain a lifetime of creative productivity.

There must be structure and steadiness if you're aiming for any kind of stable life and a successful lifestyle. You must remain grounded and centered to pursue your purpose over the long haul and not flame out.

Purpose is not a high, whereas passion is.

Flow is not a high either, it's a deep feeling of absorption meets peace and inspiration and challenge that feels really good, but is not fiery like passion.

Purpose is a very grounding force. It has a stability to it that tethers you to the earth. Whereas passion will send you soaring over the heavens as if you can fly.

Purpose allows a moderate healthy lifestyle and encourages plenty of sleep, good eating, sober clean living and positive drama-free relationships. Purpose understands that illness, drama, addiction, out-of-your-mind relaxation, pulling all nighters, insomnia, eating like crap and not exercising all keep you from being at your peak state of focus and effectiveness.

Passion is dangerous because you often try to stimulate it or recreate it using addictive substances that take you away from your Soul. The Ego loves drugs and alcohol as distractions from your Soul's purpose.

Purpose pulls you back in when you go off-center or stray from your path. You might get busy or swamped with other things, or experience a loss or life change that is going to take you a minute to recover from. Purpose patiently waits and calls to you without shame or guilt. It knows that you will come back to it.

Purpose understands that at certain times in your life you're not going to be able to pay it that much attention, like after you have a baby and for the next three years or so. Purpose loves that idea, it will just incorporate your new role as a parent into the mission. Parenting and relationships are great motivators for living a purpose-driven life.

Passion is far more demanding, it's a very jealous and possessive lover.

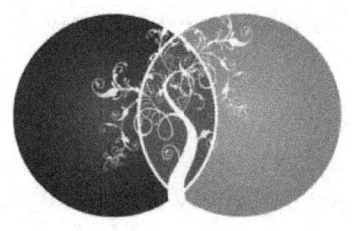

SEEK AGAIN

Once my book was out and I was largely over the postpartum depression and burnout the question still remained, what do I do now without my Soul's purpose?

Do I just get another one? Do I get a free pass now and I don't have to be compelled to any other Soul-driven acts that drive me to burnout and illness? Is my purpose now just to market and promote that book and get it to all the hands I can?

What now Soul?

Those were my questions for several months.

However, before that the postpartum was so painful and exhausting that I just said fuck it and took my kids to Mexico for a month.

I was quite happy to have my purpose be to sit on the beach and watch the waves roll in and bathe in the womb of Mother Earth swimming with her great beasts, the whale sharks, and hanging out with my kids with no schedule.

Of course, I never would have said fuck it and taken a month-long vacation with my kids had my business and my health not been so shitty. I was only willing to do it because I had nothing to lose. My Soul had told me to get out of town before, but I hadn't said YES! Not until things got drastic. Sound familiar?

So as I recovered in Mexico I allowed my mind to wander and relax. I wrote and wrote in my journal asking hard questions, big questions.

What is the point of all this?

I'm back to this question, I thought, how can I be back at this fucking question? I thought I had so much figured out with the Law of Attraction and saying YES! to my Soul, how had I come back to this question?

The secret of getting answers to the big questions such as these lies somewhere in getting comfortable staying in the question and letting go of the answer. Which is super unhelpfully esoteric so I'll stop saying annoying shit like that. Sorry.

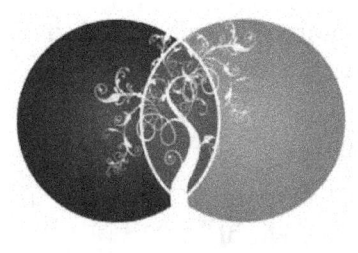

ONE SPARK

When I am asking big questions I expect the Universe to provide me with an answer. That's what Jesus promised would happen and I have found it to be true.

Two ways that I often receive answers are when I'm talking it out and writing it out. As I'm questioning and expressing about my concerns and the holes in the story and why isn't this working? and what the fuck are we doing all of this for? I often find myself answering my own questions.

It will suddenly come out of my mouth and I will hear the truth of it and it will ring a little bell of "YES!" in my Soul.

Sometimes when I'm writing something, whether marketing copy or in my journal, I will look at the page and there my answer will be. Flow-ed from Spirit onto the page through my fingers.

I wrote and wrote and wrote and wrote that whole trip in Mexico.

Then I came home and talked it out with my friend Anna. The answer spilled out of my mouth.

One spark.

We are here to bring light. It is the first command in Genesis, Let there be light.

But, how do we do that?

With one divine spark.

I had a vision of me scooting my socked feet on carpet collecting static electricity and touching the finger of someone and seeing this little spark happen between us from the electric shock of our connection.

What if it's that simple? What if there is no other big mystery and we're all making it too damned hard? I asked Anna.

One spark.
A spark between you and your lover.
A spark between you and your child.
A spark between you and the clerk.
A spark between you and the woman opening the door.
A spark between you and your client.
A spark between you and your neighbor.
A spark between you and your dog.
A spark between me and you, dear reader.
A spark between you and your Facebook friends.
A spark between you and the waitress.
A spark between you and your bestie.
What if that's your whole Soul's purpose?

SOUL vs. EGO SMACKDOWN

One Spark.

TRACEE SIOUX

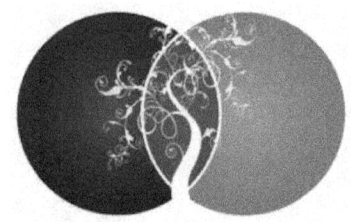

LET THERE BE LIGHT

Your Soul's purpose is to create the One Spark.

That ignites.

And builds.

Into a bigger and bigger ball of light.

Light. You hear it all the time. So many traditions reference light as being the point of creation. It's the first command in Genesis and it's a theme throughout the whole scriptural cannon.

The light is often referred to as Love.

The light is often referred to as God.

Love. God. Light.

These three themes appear interchangeably in such a variety of sources between philosophy, various world religions and traditions and cultures that there has to be an underlying truth to it. From Star Wars to Genesis to reports of near-death experiences we are instructed and encouraged to seek, create and go toward the light.

So let's assume for a moment that the whole point of humanity and the earth realm is to create light.

First God created the darkness and then he created the light. Perhaps you could say the darkness was, it existed. Then light was cast by the force of creation.

Let's agree for the moment that we have the power to create light. So what would that mean and what would that look like?

I would describe light as anything that brings joy, peace, love and happiness to the planet.

Have you met someone who you would describe as "full of light?" You know the person I'm talking about, they have a peaceful, ethereal, almost childlike joyful quality about them. You want to be around them.

To soak up their light.

Do you know that feeling I had watching that drummer? I would describe that as standing in her light.

When you stand in a museum and look at a piece of art that people have been talking about for centuries that's light.

Another way to think about it is a spark of energy. So, the static electricity between me an another person creates a new spark of energy and the energy presents itself as this little flash of light.

One spark.

Eventually one spark grows into many sparks and expands into even bigger balls of light.

Healers are often called light bringers or light workers because they use light to heal their clients. In modern medicine we know that light has a healing power as we use it to treat everything from depression to laser surgery for cancer.

We track time by how quickly light moves, the speed of light. We track the movement of our days and months by the light cast from the sun and the reflection of light on the moon.

Light, when you boil it down, is energy.

So another way to say that your Soul's purpose is to bring light, you could say that your Soul's purpose is to generate energy.

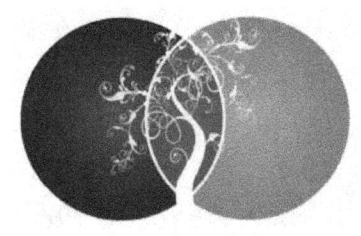

IN-LIGHT-AND-MEANING

(ENLIGHTENMENT)

Enlightenment.

We use the word enlightenment {in-light and meaning} for everything from more knowledge to more inspiration. When you have been enlightened, it's as if your brain is suddenly in a place of knowing where it was once ignorant.

We often picture this phenomenon in our culture with a lightbulb over a character's head. Suddenly, a light went on in my mind, we might say.

Have you ever had an enlightening experience? Perhaps it was similar to my porch epiphany. Where I had been experiencing a spiral into the darkness I suddenly saw a light that tempted me to follow it to create meaning in my life.

I love the moment when I learn something new, maybe something was confusing to me and I couldn't quite understand it and then—bing—the light goes on and I see everything with new eyes.

Let those with ears hear, Jesus said.

You might spend your life hearing the same messages over and over and over. Then suddenly you "get" it in a whole new way and your Soul surges with new energy, *Oh! That's what that's about.*

That's what enlightenment is. You can hear a thing over and over and over, you can even think you know a thing inside and out, but unless you experience the meaning behind it, it's not quite light.

Naturally you want to tell everyone you know about this new light you just discovered. Whether it's a new invention or a new perspective on God you want to share the light. That's exactly what you're supposed to do with it.

It feels so natural to share it because it is.

So yes, you want to help people. Most of us do. Yet, first you have to find the light, grab onto it's tail and ride it all the way to meaning.

In-Light-and-Meaning.

SOUL vs. EGO SMACKDOWN

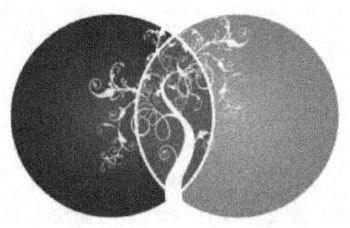

TANGIBLE SOUL PURPOSE

You're here to create one spark between you and another. So is every other Soul.

Yet, how you create that spark is personal to you and your Soul's purpose.

The means of spark creation are many and varied.

Your Soul has some preferences about how it likes to generate energy and put off fireworks in the earth realm. Not all of us gravitate towards scooting our feet on the carpet to generate static electricity and touching someone for spark creation, some of us prefer sex.

Or teaching, writing, painting, singing, mothering, relationshipping, crunching the numbers, designing dresses, putting together marketing plans, drawing cartoon characters, nursing or doctoring, mapping terrain, exploring the moon, lawyering or punditing.

You can create the spark in everything you do. The light of connection happens throughout your day while you're liking someone's baby picture on Facebook, dropping your kid off at school with an "Have a good day, I love you, see you tonight," calling your insurance guy back, answering your email, sharing a kickboxing bag with your gym friends, laying in savasana with a room full of fellow yogis, texting an old friend, meeting with your colleagues, picking up the tab at lunch, making eye contact with the checkout girl as she bags your groceries, the peck you greet your husband or wife with when they come home from work, the snuggle on the couch with your toddler, the phone call with your mom, the "hello" between you and your neighbor and the nod between you and the guy in the car turning left that says, "hey, you can go first."

Those are the sparks. One at a time, culminating in bigger and bigger light on the planet.

What I love about this definition of a Soul's purpose is that it is tangible and doable every minute of your day. You don't have to know the outcome of the spark you create between yourself and the checkout girl. You only know that it was created and it is good.

Be the change you want to see in the world, Gandhi commands on bumper stickers.

It's all on YOU! No pressure.

It sounds like a great idea at first glance. Hey, if everyone were doing this then the world would be amazing and happy and fed and safe, right? Yet, the whole world isn't doing it our Ego is quick to point out and we get all angsty and pressured when we feel like we're singularly responsible for changing the whole damn world.

But the One Spark Soul purpose doesn't hold you responsible for the outcome of the entire universe and it doesn't put all the pressure of your Soul's purpose on one single project, like a blog, book or business.

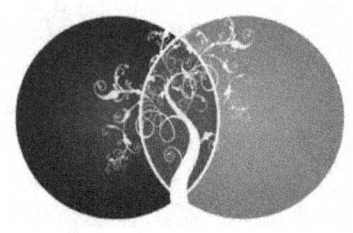

PROJECT LIBERATION

There's some real liberation in freeing yourself from feeling like your purpose is to write a book that will change the world.

Because, what if it doesn't?

What if you do tune into your Soul and you say YES! and you follow through and you write that all-important piece of literature and you pour your whole heart and Soul into it and …

No one notices.

What does that mean about your Soul's purpose?

Does it mean that it wasn't really your Soul's purpose and you were just confused and caught up in your Ego?

Does it mean that your Soul betrayed you with false promises of your book having an impact?

Does it mean that you had this one Soul's purpose and now you've gone and blown it by doing it wrong or not being able to "make it happen?"

Well, from some perspectives—and certainly your Ego's perspective—yes. It means all of that.

You failed. No one cares what your Soul's stupid purpose is. Three people read the book and one left a scathing review on Amazon that hurt your heart. You're crazy to listen to your Soul and follow the looney voices in your head that fill you with delusional fantasies of grandeur and importance.

But, if your purpose is to create a spark then the writing of this magnificent piece of literature is one project with which your Soul has used to live your purpose.

Here's how it breaks down:

The purpose is to create One Spark.

The method of spark creation is writing.

The project used to create the spark is a book.

Which means that if even one person read the book you created a spark. Even the person who left a nasty review was touched enough that they took time out of their busy life and committed energy to your creation. A spark. They may hate it, but obviously your book triggered something in them that was raw and needed healing. Though you might never know it, it is possible that the Universe used your book to trigger that healing which will change them in some fundamentally positive way.

Please note: you're not responsible for that. You did your job. You created the spark. That was your only purpose in this scenario.

Of course book production is an extensive process that involves a whole host of Souls so let's walk through how many sparks you can create by writing and publishing one book.

Remember, this book is part of your Soul's purpose.

There is you and the machine that you create on, you can picture sparks of energy being generated and shooting into the atmosphere as light as you type every single word. The act of creation and manifestation itself is more than a spark, it's more like big explosions of light that cast itself into infinity.

In the book you write about other people's ideas and that creates a spark between you and those other thinkers and authors. You write about characters and that literally brings those characters into the energy of being matter. You talk to other people about your book and that creates a spark between you and them.

Of course, you're communing with the muses and the geniuses of creativity and inspiration so sparks are flying everywhere in that process. Your Soul is traveling to the spirit realms for intel while you sleep and bringing big ginormous balls of sparkly light back with her for you to use in the creation of this book. And maybe you have a few early readers who critique it along the way and help you hammer out some of the themes and flesh out the language and there are collaborative sparks flying left and right during these interactions.

In essence you have brought what was spirit—an idea for a book—from the spirit realm and made it manifest into material matter.

It matters.

You mattered it.

That, my friends, is an act of creation.

And who creates?

God.

So what you have done so far is a miracle in and of itself.

You matter-ed.

SOUL vs. EGO SMACKDOWN

Wait, this Soul purpose project is only halfway there. Now you have to birth it into the world. You have these words on paper, but they need to find their homes out there in readers' hands.

You might start shopping the book around with agents, who then shop it around with publishers. A spark is created between you and every assistant, agent, secretary, designer, editor and publisher who touches the email, query letter or proposal.

You might choose to self publish it so needs a designer, cover artist and an editor, there too will be sparks.

Now you have to get this book into readers' hands. So you'll need publicity people and you'll need to do interviews and podcasts with reviewers and people in your industry so that people know about your book. You'll have to send out requests for all of your friends to read your book and leave reviews on Amazon and you'll post about it on Twitter and Facebook and maybe do a book signing here and there.

A spark is created between you and every single reader. You and every single person who sees your post on social media. You and every single podcast host and all of their individual listeners. A spark is created between you and everyone who glances at you sitting behind your book at a book signing, even if they don't even stop to say hello.

A spark is created between you and every eye on your marketing copy, book title or website.

This was no small task that your Soul required of you. No small task indeed.

But your Ego reminds you, there are 350,500 books published monthly on Amazon. Your book hasn't yet turned into the New York Times Best Seller of the year. It's profoundly unprofitable and you feel like it's only a drop in a sea of books.

Did your Soul fail you?

If you believe that your Soul's purpose was to sell 10 million books immediately, then yes, your Soul failed you.

But.

What if you were mistaken?

What if your Soul's purpose was really to create one spark and the creation and publication of your book created 100 sparks?

Then, my darling, you're a brilliant creative genius who just expanded light on the planet dramatically and how can that be anything but a success?

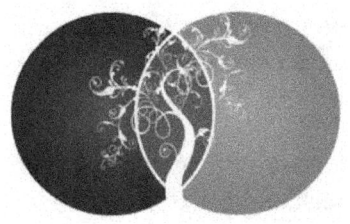

THE OUTCOME IS YOUR SOUL'S ENEMY

The outcome is your enemy, my loves.

The outcome is the Ego's game.

If you're doing the Soul project as your Soul's purpose because you're trying to get one specific outcome then you're really just setting yourself up for failure and disappointment.

The outcome is your enemy because it is out of your control.

You can influence the outcome with a multitude of doing and action and spiritual practice and mindset. To be sure we are outcome influencers.

Yet, the outcome belongs to God and the Universe.

We are very powerful players.

Still, we are very powerful players among other powerful players who are also hoping for an outcome, which might conflict with yours.

Your Soul isn't motivated by the outcome anyway, he's motivated by spark creation, experience and growth.

So often I have done this terrible crime to myself: I'll say YES! to my Soul's request that I take on a certain project, but I'll create an expectation of what that project is going to do for me.

I will write this book and it will get me on Oprah and I'll become a world class speaker and I'll have enough money to support myself and my family. My Soul wants me to do this and so that's what my reward shall be!

Um yeah. But, what if it doesn't go down like that? What if that's not the point of writing the book?

I published the book a month ago, why isn't Oprah calling?!?!?! I'm such a failure. Oh Soul, why did you do me so wrong?

What if my Soul wants me to write the book for my own healing, my own spiritual growth, my own pleasure? Because remember your Soul purpose is for your own happiness and growth. What if my Soul doesn't have any interest in this book as a means to get fame or wealth or a spot on Oprah?

Folks, probably your Soul doesn't have much interest in those things. Some Souls do, of course, but yours might not.

The outcome is the Ego's game.

The dialogue goes like this:

Soul: Hey, let's write a book about dolphins!

Ego: Hmmm, that sounds like a lot of work, what do we get out of it?

Soul: We get to learn about dolphins and maybe even swim with some and then we get to spend our days thinking about them and writing about them. I bet we could tap into some cool dolphin spirit guide energy and we'd learn a lot about being playful that way.

Ego: hmmm, I only want to do it if we can score our own television show on the Discovery Channel.

Soul: We could learn to be playful and I think Dolphins are also a symbol of creativity and love. So maybe we would learn how creativity and play lead to more love.

Ego: Hmmm, how many copies of these books do you think we can sell?

Soul: Oh and think of how much fun we could have if we made it a children's book and we worked with a talented illustrator!

Ego: Illustrators cost money.

Soul: Oh! I know! We could take some art classes and learn to draw dolphins swimming and leaping and doing tricks!

Ego: We don't know anything about drawing, what are you even talking about? Now we're going to take on an entire new art form for this money-sucking project? We don't have the time or the money for this stupid project.

Soul: Gaaaaa! I'm trying to bring happiness here! Why do you have to say no to everything?

Ego: Fine, I'll do it as long as you can promise we'll sell 10 million copies, make $100 million dollars and get our own show on the Discovery channel and it costs nothing to produce.

The outcome is the Soul's enemy. The outcome is the Ego's game.

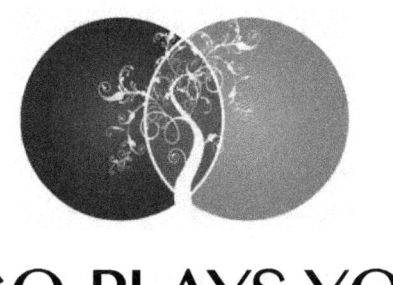

EGO PLAYS YOU

Let's talk about how badly your Ego needs you to stay in Same and how far he's willing to go to keep you stuck.

This is a primordial creature within the most ancient part of your brain, remember? His concept of time is hunting in the daytime and being home before dark so the wild animals don't eat him. He wants to minimize socializing with other foreign tribes, only trading what he has to because he desires to be as self-reliant as possible. All other people and animals are dangerous.

He wants to follow the same routine day in and day out to minimize his risk. Rise at sunrise, gather, hunt and make sure all work is done by twilight and head back to the cave to root and sleep. This guy is still terrified of fire and doesn't know what a wheel is. Those inventions require experimentation and adventure and he is just not down with that. His Soul's purpose, if he were to ever consider such an elevated subject, is to stay alive; beating starvation, animal attack and freezing to death. He'd like to have sex every once in a while, but he's not sure why since he has not yet discovered that sex leads to propagation of the species, so he's not so great at romance and courtship yet either. His vocabulary is also quite limited, often resorting to name calling and banging you over the head with this trusty stick. Avoid risk. Stay alive.

Let's talk about his perspective of how you spend your time.

You stay up after dark.

You interact with way too many people.

You speak to strangers.

You drive a car.

You fly in planes.

You want to buy and sell more than you need to survive.

You use money which is too abstract and intangible to depend on.

You're at the mercy of political systems that are unreliable and intrusive.

You don't get enough sleep.

For the Ego everything about you is weird and terrifying. We know from Maslow's Hierarchy of Needs (Abraham Maslow was a groundbreaking psychological researcher of human motivation and happiness) that this guy is on the lowest two needs levels. Maslow teaches us that before we even have an evolutionary consciousness that can conceive, let alone yearn for, a Soul's purpose we must have our fundamental survival needs met.

Maslow illustrated our human needs in the form of a triangle with the bottom being the lowest level and the peak of the pyramid being the highest. The needs have to be achieved on one level in order to progress to the next level. They go in this order: physiological needs (breathing, food, water, shelter, clothing, sleep); safety and security (health, employment, property, family and social stability); love and belonging (friendship, family, intimacy, sense of connection); self-esteem (confidence, achievement, respect of others, the need to be a unique individual); self-actualization (morality, creativity, spontaneity, acceptance, experience, purpose, meaning and inner potential).

So you see, even opening this book and reading page one signifies that you are on, or at least toying with, the top tier of human evolution and consciousness, while your poor Ego is still fixated on the bottom tier.

Think about that for a second. In order for you to even have the luxury of contemplating and asking the question, "what is my Soul's purpose?" you have to have achieved a level of human comfort and affluence, as well as self-awareness and personal growth, for the question to even exist in you.

Take a bow; I'm applauding you right now.

Still, here's the thing, your Ego is never going to grow out of level one or two: physical safety and security needs. Ego's concern will always remain breathing, food, water, shelter, clothing and sleep first.

But because he suspects your affluence and your higher level ambitions he has become an expert at holding you hostage with the fears listed in level two: health, employment, property, family and social stability. I'm pretty sure the Ego isn't actually on this level two, but he's aware of its impact and importance to you, so he uses it to ensure his primary level one needs.

So here's how the inner conflict goes for most of us:

Soul: Oh I'm so excited to write this book about dolphins, I think we're so connected to them in this higher consciousness spiritual way and I think we can learn a lot from them about how to telepathically communicate and there's some psychic phenomenon that they can teach us about. I think what I'll do is take off every Friday to focus on my Dolphin research and take a few trips to some really cool dolphin research facilities who are engaging in some ground breaking research in the next few months. Then I'll take a six-month hiatus from my job to write the book and hire a publicist to really get it out there. This is going to be so exciting!

SOUL vs. EGO SMACKDOWN

Ego: Oh my God, you can't do that! What are you, fucking crazy? You're going to be a terrible mother if you put all this time into one stupid book and your boss is not going to give you an hiatus! He will fire you in a heartbeat and no one wants to read such a stupid book and then we'll be publicly humiliated as the stupid woman who wrote a book about something no one cares about who got fired and made her children hate her from sheer neglect and then we'll die broke and alone!!!

See how using that first and second tier of needs against you can really work to keep you stuck in your same job, doing your same parenting schedule and never stepping out into a higher Soul calling?

Your Ego is no amateur. He's been practicing this game for lifetimes and he's got you pegged cold.

He's really quite genius.

Which means that you and your Soul have to learn his favorite plays and develop a game plan to outsmart his trusty tactics, which have been working on you for so very long.

Sister, Brother, your Ego's been playing you.

TRACEE SIOUX

SLAVE MASTER

Once I get this work done everything will be okay and then I can focus on my Soul's purpose.

I want to grab people by the shoulders and shake them when people tell me this lie. It's as if they are a record player stuck on that one grating lyric.

Because that is what this is, just a stuck record repeating over and over and over.

I don't have enough time.

There's no truth anywhere in this statement.

It's just a big fucking lie.

And who's the liar?

You guessed it.

Ego.

I don't have enough time.

It's the Ego's biggest and most effective lie. He's so freaking good at this lie that he has everyone in the Western world repeating it. This is his #1 platinum hit. I thought maybe other cultures were escaping this one, but I went to Mexico and they were playing this hit tune there too.

> *I Can't.*
> *So busy.*
> *Too busy.*
> *Crazybusy.*
> *Someday I'll have more time.*
> *When things settle down.*
> *After this project.*
> *As soon as this happens.*
> *If I only had more time.*
> *When I have more time,*
> *THEN I'll do what I want to do.*

No, you won't.

Do you know how I know that? Because you don't have a time problem. You have an Ego problem.

You can't solve an Ego problem with more time, or a better calendar system or a time management program. All of those tools will just help you fill up your time with yet more bullshit that keeps you away from your Soul's purpose.

Because remember what the Ego's motivating factor is? SAME. So if you have more time, he'll just keep you busy doing more of the same. He won't be making more time available for doing any changey, scary Soul purposing, no, there will be none of that crazy talk. If you are not the master of your time you are the master of nothing. That's what I tell my clients. But, here I'm willing to take it a step further.

If your Soul is not the master of your time, *your Ego is*. For the vast majority of the Western world Ego is the Master of Time.

He's a genius at it. He's not playing a kids' game anymore, he has the clock wrapped around your balls and you feel the clenching of his fist daily with increasing pressure.

OUCH! Part of the reason the Ego so easily claimed time as his domain is that the Soul understands that time is an illusion invented by humans so they can meet each other for coffee at the same moment.

The Soul's purpose rarely comes with a timetable deadline because time doesn't really exist.

Oh, but the Ego loves time. It's such a masterful weapon in its game against the Soul.

First the Ego loves to keep you busy, late and rushing.

You can practically see him rubbing his hands in wicked delight as he subtly keeps you running from one place to the other so that you literally "don't have time to think," especially about your Soul's purpose.

Yes, you're always on the run and never have any time and that's just perfect for Ego who knows that the Soul's voice has often been referred to as the "still small voice" and that you have to slow down, get still and listen for you to hear it.

When are you going to have time to do that?

You're just too crazybusy for sitting still and getting quiet enough to hear your Soul whisper some crazyass plan into your gullible ear.

Brilliantly played Ego. He's been doing this so masterfully to some of you that you haven't even noticed for decades. Decades!

That's not his last move in Time chess. Not even close, Bud.

He's also exceptionally good at filling the calendar with important things. Because your job as a person is to be everything to everyone that means that all appointments, engagements and obligations involving other people are important.

Leaving ... *nothing* for your own Soul's purpose.

Check.

Oh, I know love, it is so important to be at every soccer practice and every single book club, and all the church potluck functions and every single networking lunch in town and plan every friends' birthday or else *you'll lose your job no one will like you and you'll die alone.* Remember?

Ah, but now that you know this dirty trick, you can just develop a better calendar and a time management system and smoosh your Soul's purpose in there somewhere.

Heeheehee, the Ego giggles behind his squirrelly hand. **It's time to bring out the long line of "emergencies and shit that can go wrong" moves. I can keep her hopping from crisis to crisis and drama to drama for decades before she even suspects.**

Suddenly, you're having dramatic encounters with customers and subcontractors and coworkers that were never there before. Your spouse and children begin to revolt at the slightest hint of change emerging. Friends start thinking you're getting too big for your panties at the slightest mention of upcoming Soul projects you mention.

Your body begins to develop ailments and kinks, injuries and sicknesses as the Ego manipulates it like a puppet on strings. Not enough to kill you, of course, but enough to keep you from making any surges forward with your newfangled Soul purpose plans.

Ego knows that drama, illness and crisis are fantastic distractions and that no Soul purposing will fit in even the best time management system if your life is mired in them.

Check mate.

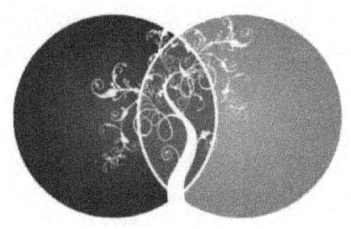

SOUL-FULL TIME

While your Soul may not care too much about time, you as the Self better start taking this war on your time very seriously for the reasons I just mentioned.

It's actually a very dangerous game with real stakes, including your physical and mental health, relationships, career and business. Not to mention any higher gratification you might be looking for from being able to live your Soul's purpose.

It's time to take back the clock and become master of your time. This isn't going to be the easiest thing you've ever done, but it will be a life-changer if you do it consistently.

I have a 10 class ecourse, Time Joy-gasm in my Maxcelerator's group coaching program, which will change your entire relationship to time if you follow the steps, more info here, http://traceesioux.com/maxcelerators-mastermind/.

TRACEE SIOUX

For now, I'm going to give you as much of the info here as I can without straying too far off our topic.

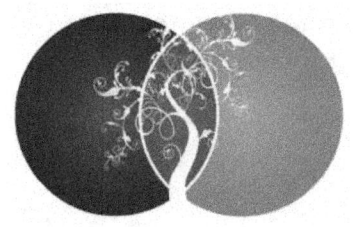

TIME JOY-GASM

We frequently hear people say, "Oh I wish I had more time." Maybe this is one of your go-to one liners.

No. You. Don't.

Like you need one more hour to fill with work and other important tasks the Ego has laid out for the time you already have now.

What you really wish is that you <u>experienced your time in ways that made you happier</u> and gave you more pleasure.

You don't want more time.

You want to spend your time doing things you love doing and things that are truly important to you.

You want more time to live your Soul's purpose. To create the One Spark in ways that bring your Soul more meaning and joy.

TRACEE SIOUX

So let's look at some ways that you can create a Time Joy-gasm in your own life.

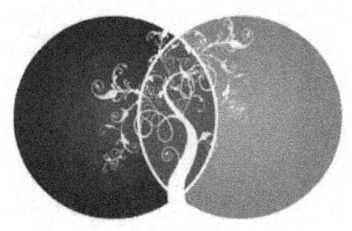

PLEASURE DRENCHING

Do you ever wonder why your Soul wanted to manifest into a human body? To become physical matter in this particular shape and form?

Your Soul, unhindered by physical matter, is far more light and high vibration than your physical body.

Matter is slow and heavy.

Matter can be damaged and harmed.

Matter is vulnerable.

Human bodies are high freaking maintenance.

I've pondered this question many times and I like to believe that one of the reasons is physical pleasure.

We have many physical sensations that are unbelievably pleasurable.

Orgasms alone are probably worth manifesting a body for.

Hot baths, the smell of a baby's head, kickboxing, yoga, dancing, kissing, tasting dark chocolate, the crunch of popcorn in your mouth, the sweetness of a Jolly Rancher on your tongue, the smell of Oscar de la Renta cologne on a man, the visual appeal of wearing jewelry or a new hairstyle, holding hands, warrior one pose, whole body belly laughing, skipping, snuggling, the feel of sunlight soaking into your skin, your body being carried by the waves of the ocean, a baby nursing at your breast, sex, putting on the perfect pair of jeans, wrapping your hands around your morning cup of coffee as you watch the sunrise, the smell of bark and grass as you wander off a trail.

Being physical is freakin' amazing for a Soul.

It's conceivable that your Soul was partly motivated to be here for the sheer pleasure involved in being human, let's then make a leap and say that more pleasure will make you more happy.

YES! Finally some spiritual advice that doesn't require you to hold one position on a mat for 20 minutes every morning trying your hardest to think nothing.

Pleasure Drench.

I want you to put pleasure on your calendar everywhere. At least one pleasurable thing daily.

SOUL vs. EGO SMACKDOWN

I love a great book in a hot bath, reading before bed at night, yoga in the morning, kickboxing a few times a week, hiking, riding my pink cruiser bike around town, going dancing with girlfriends, meeting with my friend Anna, my regular two hour bi-Sunday massage, a mid-afternoon meditation nap, sex, kissing, binge-watching Netflix, buying a new dress and a million other things that make my Soul sing. And yes, my Soul sings during all of these activities.

What is pleasurable to you? Do that. Often. Indulge in pleasure, drench yourself in it.

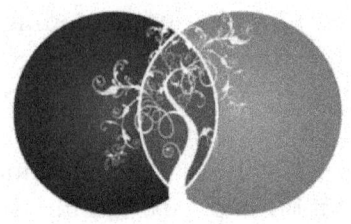

EASY vs. HARD

During my divorce I had a rough summer. I plunged into poverty. I was making $600 a month and feeding my kids from the food bank. I was rushing, rushing, rushing everywhere I went in the belief that the harder and faster I worked the more I would get done and the more money I would make.

Slow down, I kept hearing my Soul's voice whisper. *Slow down.*

I rushed so fast that I got three tickets, two for speeding and one for not stopping at a stop sign.

Slow down.

I fell down some stairs rushing from a massage to a medical appointment. Still I did not slow down.

SLOW DOWN.

One day I was rushing to the park, for no real reason except that rushing was my default state, when I flew off my daughter's pink Barbie razor scooter and broke my clavicle.

That's when I finally slowed down long enough to hear my Soul's voice. It was forced on me. I thought I would just get up and go about my business in the morning, maybe take an afternoon nap. That is not how it went down. I was in excruciating pain and I wasn't allowed to push, pull, move or carry anything over five pounds. I was in so much pain that I couldn't think, I couldn't work.

Funny thing. My inability to do what I had been doing was a brilliant turn of events in that I had to figure out a new plan. At the time I was doing crappy piece writing work. I had all of these assignments due but they paid pennies and I was barely scraping by, yet I had no time left to take on more work. I couldn't rush fast enough to resolve the fundamental problem. I was out of time and I didn't have enough money.

It was a conundrum.

When I broke my clavicle my work ethic wouldn't allow me to miss my deadlines though I was incapable of completing the assignments.

I hired someone to finish them for me.

I kept part of the pay.

Hey, I think I just stumbled onto how people end up creating empires, I thought.

My whole paradigm about my place in the business world and the marketplace shifted.

As primary breadwinner, I no longer had the luxury if petering around in my business and doing crappy paying piecework. I needed a new plan and that plan had to have me as the employer paying others to do much of the work.

In other words, I flew off my pink Barbie razor scooter as a starving artist and stood up a businesswoman and entrepreneur.

You know what I think?

I think my Soul had been giving me the secret all along. I had already started hiring some help for other projects, but I was refusing to slow down and listen long enough for her to really give me the answer to my own desperate plea, *help me.*

I've seen it time and again, sometimes when you're refusing to listen, even though you're begging for help, your Soul will insist that you listen because she came here to do something and you're not doing it, damn it!

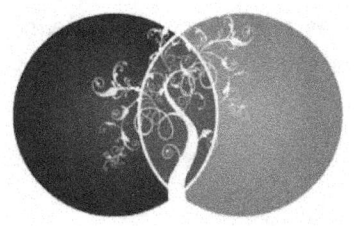

TIME TITHE

When I started my Year of YES! experiment one of the first things that my Soul told me to do was to get healing work done on myself. I was turning forty, had just finalized my divorce and I was in desperate need of healing.

I started buying massages on discount websites. I'd buy a $15 or $30 massage and it was okay. Except you get what you pay for. A massage can be a simple rub down or it can be a profoundly healing experience.

Tithe here, my Soul started saying while I was on massage tables getting a rub down. *Tithe here, to this piece of God.*

The tithe is traditionally a ten percent donation to a church or the place where you are being spiritual fed. I grew up with the principle of tithe and had tithed to a church the prior year as a Law of Attraction manifestation tool.

Now my Soul was telling me very clearly to, tithe here, to this piece of God.

Your body is the temple of the Spirit who lives in you, Jesus told his followers.

I AM.

Remember? My Soul is the piece of me that is God. As is yours.

So I committed to tithing ten percent of every dollar that came to me to my own Soul's healing.

I also committed tithing ten percent of my time to my own Soul's healing.

What a fabulously healing year which transformed everything. By putting my self-care in my budget and on my calendar first it changed how I lived my life. It changed the health and energy level of my body, it changed my emotional and mental ability to care for my children and manage my responsibilities and it completely transformed my business into one of profit and legit entrepreneurship versus just playing around for extra income as I had as a stay-at-home-mom.

The Time Tithe changes everything.

Your Ego is going to hate it.

Do it anyway. Because when you put your Soul first all the other stuff falls into place. You get healthier, you get more physically fit, you have more fun, your business grows, you feel happier and you start spending your time living your Soul's purpose in a very gratifying and organic way.

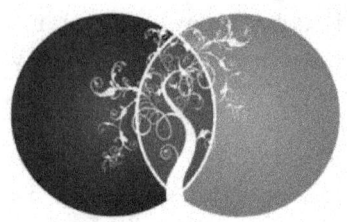

TRUE VALUES FIRST

If you want to create more time in your life—meaning more pleasure in your time—put your true values on your calendar first. If you're committed to your Soul's purpose then related activities go on the calendar before other obligations.

Haven't you noticed already that what you try to squeeze into your calendar last is the thing that gets squeezed out first?

Do you believe your Soul came here for a purpose?

Do you have a desire to fulfill that purpose?

Then put it on there first.

I know right now some of you are looking at your schedule and you want to scream about the impossibility of spending ten percent of your time pampering yourself and putting that time on the calendar first.

Ok. Scream.

Done?

Then let's get to the word NO.

Right now you are making choices. You might not be completely cognoscente of what your choices are, but you are making them by default nonetheless.

You've been saying yes to other people's agendas for your life. Whether that's a spouse, boss, kid, friends, neighbors or family there are too many YESes floating around your calendar that should be Nos.

Those Nos are important because that's what makes room for the Soul's Yeses.

Here's an example of what I mean: when I was a young mother I felt all this pressure to be the perfect mother. I would pursue my profession as a writer, but only after all the perfect mothering was done. I wouldn't allow it to interfere with taking care of my children. I would do all the carpooling, all the cleaning and all the parenting. I would make sure that I didn't let "other people" raise my kids. Oh no, not me. I was raised Mormon and good Mormons do not let other people mother their children so that they can pursue their own ambitions. I was teetering over the line to have any professional writerly ambitions at all. My Ego was convinced that even dabbling was too much risk and it put me through hella Inner Mommy War struggles to even pursue the calling at all.

After my divorce, I was suddenly mother and primary breadwinner and I knew I better get my professional shit together to support my kids.

Still, I faced this horrible scheduling problem. My daughter had to be at school at 7 am, my son didn't have to be there until 9 am, then my daughter got out at 2:30 pm, then my son got out at 4 pm. I was determined to keep physically fit so I needed to go to the 9:15 yoga and kickboxing classes. Then there were the after school kid activities that I was responsible for driving them to and from.

By the time I got everyone to school and worked out I could run my business between 11 am and 2 pm. Then squeeze an hour of work in after I picked up my daughter but before my son got home.

I could devote three hours completely guilt-free to my business without infringing on my personal definition of motherhood and my personal commitment to my body.

Dear reader, you are allowed to change your definitions and make new plans and new priorities and new commitments.

Do that now.

I really needed to make the money generating activities a more prominent feature on my calendar NOW. What was sucking up all my time?

Driving kids.

What is sucking up your calendar? You know who you are. Neglecting your Soul's purpose in favor of a menial driving position. Don't you dare tell me that this is your quality time. I've been in that car. I know what goes on in there is not out of some after school special about how close parents and children can be. You're rushing and frustrated and so are they, everyone is hungry and everyone is tired.

Truly, this was not my favorite part of parenting. In fact, it's my most loathed part of parenting.

I don't want to spend my life in a car driving to watch other people live their lives. There, I said it.

Because parents, let me be clear on this. Watching other people develop skills and talents and live their purpose is not the same as developing your own skills and talents and living your own purpose, even if they're your children.

Having established that playing chauffeur is not my Soul's purpose and therefore not my True Value, I negotiated for my co-parent to hire someone to take my daughter to and from school and pick up some of the after school activity driving.

This added three or four hours to my workday. My income now reflects that.

I don't know what kinds of should-be-nos are filling up your calendar. I don't know what choices you're going to make about your time, but I know that they need to be made in a conscious and intentional way. You're going to have to take a really hard look at your calendar and ask yourself whether each activity is your true value, your real priority. If it's not, you'll need to start saying No in service to your Soul's purpose or you'll never have time to live it at all.

Which means that you're going to have to disappoint some folks.

But, your Soul won't be one of them and soon you'll realize how great that feels.

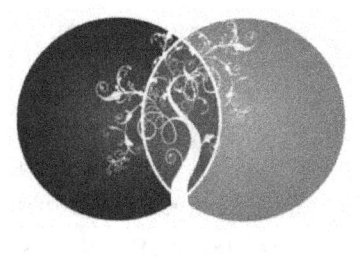

ONE CHOICE

When people make choices it takes a considerable amount of brain power. Remember our Ego and how much he enjoys the same routine over and over and over? You're wise to make use of that characteristic to keep him calm. You'll always get more done (and enjoy it more) when the Ego isn't throwing a tantrum.

"Spontaneity" is in the upper levels of our needs, which means it takes quite a bit of planning and organization for you to feel safe and stable enough to be spontaneous. Spontaneity isn't a lifestyle or a personality or character trait, it's more of an isolated event that happens irregularly, otherwise it's not spontaneous.

I enjoy spontaneity as much as the next free-wheeling creative person, but it's really not your Soul's game. Souls by nature are intentional.

You know that whole thing where spiritual people get to be flighty and directionless and change their mind all the time and change professions like they change underwear because they can't commit because their Souls are so carefree?

Forget it. Their Egos have just figured out how to trick them into thinking they're being Soul-full when really they're just being directionless and unproductive. It's a favorite means of Ego-distraction for the spiritual types who like to believe they're following their Soul by getting nothing done.

Don't fall for that.

Egos are harmless if they don't feel threatened and one of the most stabilizing and comforting things you can do to keep the Ego from messing with your Soul's purpose is to create a stable structure for your life.

When you do your Soul-creative activities as a routine, the Ego eventually puts it in the "same" category and therefore the "safe" category. Eventually he stops freaking out and sabotaging it.

Bodies, minds and emotions thrive on structure and routine. Creativity thrives on structure and routine. Professional creatives like designers and writers know that if they sit down to create at the same time every morning that the geniuses of inspiration will inevitably show up during that time.

People who don't know this believe that they'll just write that book when inspiration strikes. What a dumb idea. Inspiration comes when people make space for it to come.

SOUL vs. EGO SMACKDOWN

People who are fit and healthy understand that keeping a regular exercise schedule and eating plan is the secret. It's not bursts of hyper-exercise and a strict diet when they feel too fat that keep them in shape. They make sure that they have what they need built into their life. Someone who writes the same exact exercises in their calendar, same time, same days, from week to week will see better health and fitness results than someone who takes a run every now and then. My kickboxing classes have remained on the same dates and times of my calendar for five years. My yoga times are flexible and therefore I don't do yoga consistently.

The secret to enforcing consistent habits is to make one choice. I don't ask myself a new question every Monday, do I want to go to kickboxing? because I've already decided that I do go to kickboxing every Monday at 12:15 pm. That is sacrosanct. For anyone who asks to fill that spot in my calendar, I say, Sorry, I'm already booked. My Soul is super vocal during my kickboxing class and my body craves the fierceness of movement, there's no way I'm allowing other people to infringe on this Soul time. And my Ego? Well, she really likes to kick the shit out of a bag so she doesn't argue much with my Soul during that hour. It's a blissful hour inside myself where everyone is in agreement. It's sacrosanct. Nonnegotiable.

People who own their own companies and become successful also keep regular hours and get great at what they do. No serious entrepreneur works at random hours in their sweat pants. It's a dumb idea. That person is just unemployed. A serious entrepreneur understands what their time limitations are and they have goals and ambitions that fit between those hours.

People who have steady strong relationships also create structure around their schedules. They do not rely on "see you when I see you" to create strong bonds. They reserve time for each other and they know that it has to be both frequent and meaningful if they want the relationship to thrive.

People who are great divorced co-parents don't do a random parenting plan. Each parent knows exactly what their days and times are and they create a stable parent-child schedule that allows the kids to feel stable and safe even though they are going back and forth.

People who meet their own goals and expectations have the sense to create a schedule for even creating their goals and expectations. They usually ritualize it in some way. Every year, for instance, my family and I host a Dream Board party for our like-minded intentional friends. At that party we sit down and creatively ask our Soul's what we want for the coming year. Some of the goals and ambitions are tangible and others are more subjective. However, we don't ever say, oh this year let's have the party in April. No. The ritual is calendarized the during week after New Year's, it's built into the yearly cycle.

Our holidays are built into the yearly cycle and our personal energy levels wax and wane with the earth's natural cycles as well. Learn to use that rather than resist it.

I'm telling you that about 80 percent of success is just consistency. The things that you consistently plan and make one choice about are the things that will see the most success in your life.

If you want to live your Soul's purpose instead of just planning to "someday," this is the kind of choice-making and commitment it's going to take to make it happen.

TRACEE SIOUX

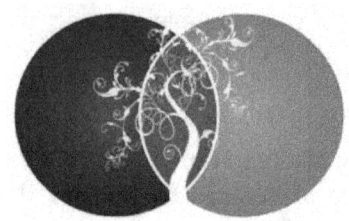

WHITE SPACE SOUL'S MAGIC JUICE

Busyness is the number one killer of Soul purpose and the Ego is super genius in using it to keep you distracted and running on a hamster wheel toward nothing.

White space the Soul's magic juice.

My clients always think I'm high when I tell them that planning nothing is the most productive thing they can do for themselves. I don't mean not to plan (refer to last chapter) I mean create time in your life where nothing is the thing you're intentionally doing.

White space is an art term referring to the empty spaces on a canvas. It's the space around the focal point objects that allow the eye to rest. Think of a painting of a barn. The blue sky above and around it is white space.

Look at this book even. White space is used in the margins, paragraph beginnings and at the top around the headers. I have intentionally used nothing as a creative element to add impact when I want you to focus on something significant like "One Spark." See what I did there?

Without the white space on a canvas it would overwhelm the eye and the art would bring no pleasure. Without margins, spaces or indentations in a book itwouldlooklikethisandyouwouldhaveahardtimeradingitanditwouldmakeyourbrainworktoohardandyouwouldhatethisbookpleasedonthatethisbook.

Time is the same way.

You can and should intentionally use nothing as a creative element to add impact to your life. Without it nothing will bring you joy or happiness because you'll be rushing too fast to even experience it. There will be no hearing of a Soul's voice for you to even follow.

Do you know what CEOs are finding with today's new crop of workers? Oh they are smart and productive and get very high standardized test scores. Yet, they lack a certain ability: Creativity.

Since 1950 children have been taking the Torrence Tests for Creative Thinking. In 2010, A professor at the College of William and Mary collected scores from over the last fifty years to discover that since 1990 children's creativity scores had been declining.

Children have become less emotionally expressive, less energetic, less talkative and verbally expressive, less humorous, less imaginative, less unconventional, less lively and passionate, less perceptive, less apt to connect seemingly irrelevant things, less synthesizing, and less likely to see things from a different angle, the study reported.

Some experts want to blame television and video games. Of course. Interestingly though, this generation of children is also the first in which their enrichment activities became so structured and varied that they were as busy or busier than their parents.

It seems that they never developed daydreaming and the kind of problem solving skills through free play that can only be developed one way: boredom.

It turns out that, *Mmmmmoooommmm, I have nothing to do,* is the secret magic to creativity and new ideas and out-of-the-box thinking.

That's what busyness does to your brain. It sucks up all the creativity. It stamps out imagination when all of your hours are accounted for in one "productive" activity after another.

Of course what do CEOs value most in their team? Creativity. (Well, we all know that's a little bit of a lie if you've ever suggested something to a higher up and had it shot down, but that's what they're saying).

What do Souls value most about being alive? Creativity.

Creativity does not happen in busyness.

You have to make space for it.

White space.

Which means you don't plan out every minute of every day to get everything done. You just stop doing "everything" and focus on what's most important and sometimes what's most important is nothing.

Plan nothing for Saturday.

Leave Sunday like a wide open field of possibility.

There's an entire ocean of time after six for three nights this week.

Nothing.

Glorious, creative, boring nothing.

It will feel positively indulgent, scandalous even.

During nothing your Soul will speak.

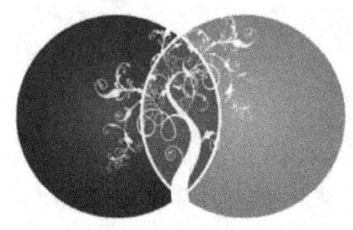

INTENTIONAL SLEEPING

A great deal of research has gone into our need and desire to sleep. As humans we come into these human bodies and we're only conscious, awake and doing stuff about half of the time. Science likes to study what we do in our sleep, are we resting or dreaming, or what?

Psychologists like Carl Jung have experimented with various levels of consciousness such as lucid dreaming. Philosophers such as Aristotle have written about it. Shamans and Tibetan monks have used it in their religious rites.

Dreams are mentioned in the Bible as prophetic, for instance when Joseph interprets the Pharaoh's dreams that predict a coming famine. There are hundreds of books about dream psychology and symbols that your subconscious mind is conjuring up in your dream states. Psychics report dreams as one of the ways they know what will happen in the future. It's a common phenomenon for people to re-experience the same dream over and over. Is déjà vu a memory of a dream or something else entirely?

If you sit down and think about it you probably have some interesting dream experiences to report. Perhaps a dream that was so vivid you swear it was real. Or you had an experience where upon waking you knew the answer to a mystery or a problem that had been eluding you when you went to bed.

Here's what I think: your Soul is doing its spiritual work while you're asleep. It's so powerful because you can't get in the way due to your Ego's unconsciousness.

I believe that your Soul travels at night on very important missions. Whether these missions aid you in your human life work or your human life work aids your Soul in its spiritual work is a paradox that I can't solve for you.

Suffice it to say that your Soul is doing work in other spiritual realms while you are sleeping.

Now, I stumbled onto this knowledge when I went to see my energy worker because I was having inexplicable feelings. I was crying and crying and crying and I had no idea why. I had racked my brain for some devastating news or terrible development or some tragic thing buried in my psyche and I came up with nothing.

So I go see my energy worker and tell her what's going on. She gets me on the table and she says, *it isn't yours.*

What? Who's is it if it isn't mine? I asked.

Your Soul had been traveling in your sleep and wasn't protecting herself and she picked up some dark energies and brought them back, she explained.

Energetic hitchhikers. Great.

We cleared them out and she helped me figure out what was happening in my sleep and how I could protect myself.

At the time this felt like something my Soul was doing to me.

Then one night my Soul woke me up because she was writing. Tap tap tap tap tap she was just writing away. I wasn't getting any rest with all the busyness up in my psyche so I woke up and said aloud, *if you're going to be working do something useful and find some people who need my help, get us some clients.*

Within a few days I was on the phone with someone who had dreamed about me. We had never personally met. She became my client.

Your Soul is out there in the ether doing work. You can ask for her assistance. Give her assignments to help you.

I will sometimes say to my Soul when she gives me a project, *Listen, I will do what you ask, write this book or take on that project, but you need to provide me with the resources I need to do it comfortably.*

SOUL vs. EGO SMACKDOWN

Which seems like an obvious request, but it's not.

Give your Soul assignments as you lay your head down to sleep. Then observe how different the world you say good night to is from the one you say good morning too.

TRACEE SIOUX

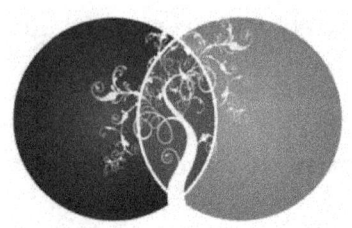

RESPECT THE MATTER

Not very many people understand that they get to require some things in return for living their Soul's purpose.

Your Soul came here for a reason.

You'll be happier if you do what she came here to do. When you say YES! to your Soul you'll feel contentment. When you say YES! to your Soul you'll probably be helping others.

All true.

But here's what happened with me for a long time.

I did my Soul's bidding faithfully, but I was broke.

Finally I got fed up with it.

I made a rule.

Yes, I made a rule for my Soul.

Respect the matter.

As we discussed, Souls aren't made of matter. They are made of high vibrational light energy. They are unhindered by bodies. If she wanted to she could put all the words in this book on the page in a blink, rather than me having to type them out by hand. Souls can travel between worlds with a millisecond thought. They can flit from earth to ether in the nanosecond that it takes you to blink. While they get pleasure from physical bodies they sometimes jet off to other planes of existence when pain is involved. They don't fully comprehend the vulnerability of human existence because matter is just play to them.

You are the matter that your Soul made physical. In a very real sense that's what you are. Matter. If you, this package of matter that it's created, die Souls just float off into the spirit realm to make themselves another body to matter in and all is well and good. They have an awareness of their own eternality that allows them to feel liberated from human nature.

Well, great for you! I shouted at my Soul one day. *But I'm matter, matter is slow and dense and it requires a hell of a lot of upkeep and maintenance. And this Earth realm trades energy in the form of MONEY and if I don't have any I can't afford to be doing your bidding and neglecting the matters of food and gas and shelter and hot water. You chose to materialize as me. So YOU need to respect the matter and help me by providing me all the resources I need including cash!*

During my Year of YES! life experiment I did a past life regression session and during that session I was allowed to play in a golden room where I could have anything I wanted. I was so happy flitting around that room with amazing breasts and glowing skin and all the beautiful things that I could have simply if I wanted them.

When my spiritual guides told me it was time to go back to earth, I grabbed a stack of money—one million dollars—and stuck it in the gold clutch I happened to be carrying. I got almost to the door and thought better of it, I went back and grabbed another million, stuck it in my clutch and turned around and shouted,

Don't you act like you don't know this matters down there!

Because yeah, money matters down here. And so do a lot of other resources, including time and love. So I'm going to need more of all three if you don't want me to quit doing this work and go get a job at the Screaming Peach waxing vaginas all day and bringing home a steady paycheck.

That's generally how my Soultematum goes. Is that Ego? Maybe, but the Soul really does need reminding sometimes that it's not the only one that matters.

If your Soul can materialize itself into a human body it can also matter up some money energy to sustain itself in a human body and make the Ego feel safe so you're not in a panicked freaked out crisis all the time. That's fair.

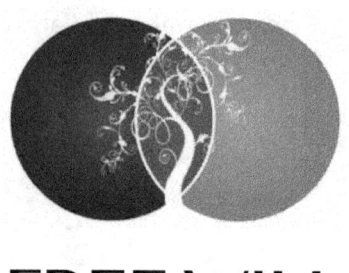

FREE WILL

So, the Ego keeps you alive with its primordial survival brain and the Soul made you matter and has this big higher spiritual agenda so what are you?

I mentioned before that you are the Self. You're the combination of both Soul and Ego, but I think you're more than that. You're a third distinct energy which contains the personality and characteristics and preferences and idiosyncrasies and maybe you contain the gifts and talents that you can develop to help the Soul serve its purpose.

You're born with gifts and talents, but it's only the persistent practice and discipline and commitment that develop those into anything marketable or worthwhile. I suppose that's the Self's job.

But you have a separate and distinct power that you hold over both the Soul and the Ego.

Free Will.

Notice that in the last section I told you how I got really sick of sacrificing my earthly material needs for my Soul's purpose and finally refused to do it?

That's free will.

It took me a long time to understand that I could use it to stand up for myself, even against the spiritual side of myself.

I work with many healers and I adore them. I feel like there's an awakening on the planet happening and there are many brilliant, powerful and gifted healers who are here to help us. So it's such a privilege to be the one who helps them figure out how to turn their spiritual gifts into profitable businesses.

A lot of that job is just trying to convince them to not be the slaughtered lamb for their Soul's purpose.

Listen to me.

Don't be the slaughtered lamb.

Get paid.

SOULPRENEUR

Can you expect your Soul's purpose to be your full time, bread on the table job?

There's not one straight answer to that question. Don't you wish there were?

I believe you can make a living using your Soul's purpose. How that works and what it looks like will morph and change over time. For me it has taken a variety of shapes and sizes and for you it will too. So don't make it so narrow that it suffocates you. Remember that living your Soul's purpose is supposed to bring you happiness and pleasure.

Your Soul understands that money is a collective agreement of all Souls on earth for generations now. So it's no surprise to it that a living must be earned. Which is why I believe that your Soul's purpose can probably made into a wage earner.

I have always been determined to live by my pen. Of course, I've met writers who will declare that they won't sell their Soul out to write marketing copy or be a poorly paid journalist or hawk their talents writing tag lines for corporations.

I guess you're opting for the day job option then.

Because I have done all of those things with my pen. My career started in journalism and took a couple of crash and burn turns along the way as journalism tried to die and be resurrected. I have written hundreds of blogs for corporations and small businesses and even for content farms. I've written tag lines and marketing copy for industries such as processed chicken and pipe fittings and tomato seeds and engineering firms. I've written LinkedIn profiles and thousands of social media posts.

Was all of that my Soul's purpose?

All of that writing made me better at the writing craft itself. It's been part of the 10,000 hours of practice that has made me excellent at what I do.

It pays my bills.

My Soul insisted that I pursue writing and I couldn't not do it. I would threaten to abandon it when it got hard to make a living, but just couldn't let writing go.

This weird thing happened along the journey—My Soul led me to here.

I was studying for the LSAT when I got my first writing gig at a community newspaper making $7 an hour. I immediately abandoned my prospective law career. There wasn't even a second of hesitation on my part.

After another community newspaper job I realized that if I wanted to get ahead as a writer I either had to keep moving from paper to paper to advance or I had to go to the writing mecca of the Universe, New York City. In New York City I was offered two jobs right away.

The first one sounded like my dream job. It was at a women's magazine, the kind they sell at the impulse magazine shelf, and I would be writing things like the fun advice column and various articles. Perfect!

The second one sounded kind of lame. It was at a business travel trade journal. I would be writing about business and sometimes there would be a free trip. The focus was on the meetings and conventions industry. Seriously?

The tie breaker was time. The first job was in New Jersey, a two-hour commute on trains between the job and my newly leased apartment in Brooklyn. I knew it wasn't sustainable. My young marriage would suffer from me never being home and I would be exhausted.

I took the business writing job.

Boy, how that has worked in my favor!

Had I taken the women's magazine job I would not be a spiritual business coach today. Talking to business owners, industry leaders, public administrators about taxes and funding and economic trends and marketing tactics became my day-to-day interest. It remained so even after that job ended and I became a freelancer.

During 20 years of business reporting I interviewed hundreds of entrepreneurs and experts in their industries to find out what they were doing. That's how I can do what I do now. I use all of that gathered knowledge to help people start their own Soul purpose companies.

Now when an energy healer comes to me wanting to create a business with her Soul purpose I can help her put together a marketing platform and create a business strategy that's going to work for her. When a real estate professional comes to me I can help her draw healthy boundaries around her time so her business doesn't eat her life, even as it gets more profitable. When someone comes to me with visions of an apparel company that is demanding to be created that won't give her any peace I know what steps to help her to take to figure out how clothes get made from vision into matter.

My Soul knew where she was going ... even though I didn't at the time.

I believe that you can use your Soul's purpose in any profession, but that your Soul obviously prefers one or a few over the rest. People have different professions over their lifetime. You might be a teacher for 25 years and then take up a second career as a healer after retirement. Several of my clients are in their retirement professions and they're as or more ambitious than my younger clients.

TRACEE SIOUX

Just remember, your Soul knows where she's going and she knows the fastest, easiest way to get there ... even if you don't.

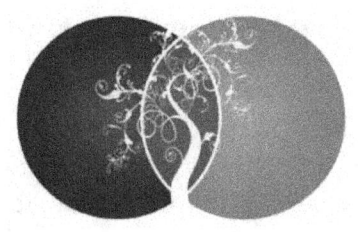

LAW OF ATTRACTION

There are lots of Law of Attraction and spiritual "get rich with positive thinking" books out there which will tell you to just visualize something and it will come to you.

If you build it they will come.

Think it and Believe it and it will Happen.

But, it's not really true is it? My client has a clear vision of the clothing line. But to make it manifest there are some steps in between visualization and manifestation that do require a little bit of know-how. In fact there are many steps.

Your Soul's purpose might have many steps that you don't know how to do too. That's okay. Because what the example of my career path shows you is that if you keep saying YES! when you get that little ding inside yourself—following it will lead you to where your Soul wants to go.

I truly thought that taking the second job back then was settling for the second best job. Yet, I find my work so fulfilling now that I wouldn't trade it for anything. Looking back I can see that the path leading me to this current career started at that fork with that choice.

My unique skill set combines the practical business information I gathered during 20 years of researching and reporting on various industries with the spiritual work I've done on myself investigating the Soul and how to manifest and attract things through spiritual law and Law of Attraction, which I started after 9/11. This combination gets results that are so unbelievable you could call them miracles.

Please note that I could never have set out at the beginning of my career after college with "spiritual business coach" as my destination. The job that I do now did not even exist when I started choosing majors. My Soul literally invented it for me as I went.

What I'm telling you is that the outcome is so incredibly unbelievably awesome that you can't imagine it, so there's no way you're going to be able to "visualize it into being."

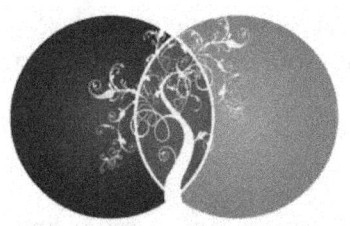

MONEY
THE BIG EXCUSE

But, Tracee, I just don't have any money.

Did you just call me on your iPhone to say that?

Oh. My. God.

We're the richest people on earth, in fact the richest civilization that has ever existed on the planet, and nobody has any money.

It's a collective mental illness.

It's absurdly untrue.

Remember when I told that after my divorce I was flat broke, making $600 a month and feeding my kids out of the food bank, doing crappy writing work that wasn't paying the bills?

Horrible, right?

TRACEE SIOUX

Poor single mothers like me, what are we supposed to do? We can't live our Soul's purpose and create dream businesses out of our delusional fantasies, right?

Can't we?

Let's look at that poor single mom again, get a closer view at the whole picture and try to figure out how the hell she did make a dream business out of her delusional fantasy.

There she is, standing in line at the food bank with her young six-year-old son who thinks of this place as the "free food store," and he helps her fill their bags with some fresh veggies, day-old bread and barely expired dairy.

She tries not to check her iPhone while standing in line so as to not inappropriately flash a symbol of wealth. She notices that most of those in line do have smart phones.

She drives away in her paid for 2005 deluxe minivan, with leather seats and heated booty warmers, to her home which she now independently owns and has the lowest mortgage in town because they bought before the next boom.

She and her children buy their designer clothes primarily from the thrift store but people regularly ask her for style advice because it's not about how much you spend it's about how you wear it.

She pays her subcontractors to do the work as she seeks bigger projects for her company. She spends all of her money on learning new business models and strategies that might work for her. She invests every extra penny into her business, in faith that it will pay off and create a better life for her family. Which is, if you recall, how every American dream story begins.

She prioritizes her health because she knows that without it she's in real trouble. So she spends money on massages, energy work, healthcare, supplements and a gym membership.

She refuses to get a job because her Soul whispers, *If you do not throw yourself into this business we will get stuck here and we cannot get stuck here.*

She can see that if she takes a customer service job to pay the bills she will be trapped in the low-pay-always-scraping-by-never-getting-ahead lifestyle and she won't have time to build her business.

There's this voice telling her that if she just keeps following this voice, she'll be led to the light.

The light of love, happiness and belonging.

The feeling of waking in the morning and knowing that there's a reason to bother trying.

The feeling that she matters.

She can feel the exciting creation energy as she matters her book and her business into existence.

She has the joyful experience of creating the spark.

So you don't have any money?

Yeah, me either.

Neither do the majority of people who currently live their Soul's purpose.

Ask any American on the street, we're broke, we don't have any money and we don't have enough time.

So what?

The secret of living your Soul's purpose is not about waiting for the moment when you have enough time or when your bank account has enough zeros for you to do it without stress.

The secret of living your Soul's purpose is insistence.

You insist that the Universe provide the way, then it must.

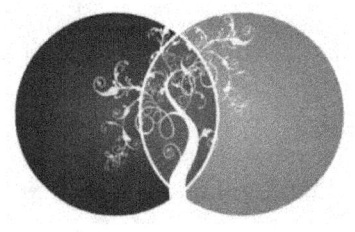

SOULCONOMICS

Money.

There is not a more highly charged issue than money. The word itself can induce magnificently passionate reactions in people.

The Bible says, *The love of money is the root of all evil,* boy has this one been used to demonize both money and love. Even as the church begs you for 10% of yours.

Here's the thing about money. Most of it is imaginary. It isn't even in the form of matter. Of the $10.5 trillion American dollars circulating in the world, only $1.2 trillion is in cash and coins. The other trillions are just numbers in machines.

What is money even?

Money is energy.

Every country and culture on the planet has agreed—for the sake of convenience—to exchange energy for goods and services rendered in the form of money.

Dude, it's hard to send your family chicken to China in exchange for a cheaply made party dress.

Money is convenient.

Money is also a Universal Soul Agreement.

Think of the collective consciousness that has gone into the agreement that money is the primary means of energy exchange all over the planet for many generations. For thousands of years all Souls have come here understanding that money is our energy currency.

So what would make such energy evil?

Like love and God, the energy of money can be distorted and abused by people.

I have a client who says things like, rich people are greedy and not generous.

Really? Because poor people are virtuous and generous? As a rule?

More likely stingy people are those who have a sense of fear and lack in their lives and generous people have a sense of abundance and gratitude in their lives and it has little to do with the amount of money in their bank account.

Money can be used to create light.

Money can be used to feed the dark.

Money itself is simply energy to be used by humans.

Spiritual people often turn their noses up at money believing all sorts of nonsensical stereotypes about what kind of people have money, what motivates people to get it, what people have to sacrifice to get it and what people do with it.

People with money are not "spiritual enough," are motivated by greed, have to work themselves to the bone and sell their Souls to make it, spend it on ridiculously unworthy things and are not grateful enough for it.

Money hate is a bullshit Ego move.

What's the biggest thing that can set you free to live your Soul's purpose?

Money.

Money allows you to finance the purpose. Businesses cost money to grow. Kids cost money to raise, feed and house. Love affairs and marriages without money tend to end in conflict over money.

Poor people are often more obsessed with money than rich people. They are all-consumed with not having money, worrying over their bills, resentment that they can't meet their basic needs and frustration every time they buy something or have an unexpected expense.

Their Egos lie to them telling them that this is somehow about their worthiness, that they are incapable of earning money because of their circumstances, their value to the world is less than rich people's and they are more holy than those having an easy life full of riches.

No.

Money is Reciprocal.

Re-cycle-able, if you will.

Let's follow the sparks that money creates.

You own a Soul purpose-driven company. Let's say it's that cycling apparel company. This product has harassed you and demanded that you create it. So you muster up everything you've got and you do it.

During the process you hire various people to help you: apparel designers, a business coach, people to help you with your marketing and website. Each of those people are running their own Soul purpose-driven businesses that you've just helped succeed and stay in business. Now those people go out and spend the money on mortgages and groceries, which is given to the checkers and bank employees who can now use to spend the money. So many sparks!

You have to buy products to create and sell your clothes. This puts money in the pocket of clothing designers, manufacturers, sewing machine operators, packagers, the post office or UPS employees and every person who comes into contact with any of the materials like thread and packing boxes. So many sparks!

SOUL vs. EGO SMACKDOWN

Now you have to sell the product to your customers, which blesses them incredibly as they feel like super heroes, pulling on their bike shorts right before a big race. Every person who sees your products, tries them on or buys them are blessed by the creation. Sparks. Sparks. Sparks.

There is a spark now between all of your employees, sub-contractors, manufacturers and customers. And these sparks aren't created with a kind word of "support," they are sparks created with energy that has real value in the world. Energy they can pay their mortgages and buy gas with. It's energy that makes their lives better.

In other words, because YOU lived your Soul purpose and started this company you thought you couldn't afford you've enabled countless others to live their own Soul's purpose and take care of their families. You've reduced their stress and made them feel valued and successful.

THAT my friends is not the root of Evil. That is LOVE and LIGHT.

TRACEE SIOUX

MONEY IS A SPARK

SOUL vs. EGO SMACKDOWN

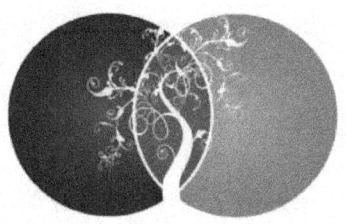

THE GAP

Mind the Gap.

That's a phrase in Britain to remind people to take care as they move from one train car to the next. Taking a tumble in the gap would prove deadly.

This seems to be the Universe's Mattering Pattern:

* Listen to your Soul.
* Say YES!
* Create an Intention
* Ask for the Universe's assistance.
* Enter the Gap.
* Watch everything you already have that you've decided to improve vanish.
* Get scared out of your mind.
* Be taunted by the Ego for making a huge mistake.
* Keep moving toward what you want.
* Start receiving what you've asked for.
* Clear the Gap
* Feel Soul-blessed.*

Like you, I have been so very pissed and afraid during this sequence of Mattering. Why, oh why, does the Universe require you to give up what you have before you get what you want?

I, like you, would much prefer to build the business before I get laid off from my current job. I, like you, would prefer to have my wealth seamlessly increase as my business instantly manifests six figures. I, like you, would much prefer to keep my current friends even as new ones come into the picture.

However, most often I find that the Universe will help you release that which is filling up your life, to make room for what you've asked for. Refer back to the importance of White Space.

Remember when you are in the gap that the Ego will take on a new fierceness, attempting to force you to turn back, making you want to hide in the cave for safety.

However, if you stay the course you'll soon make it to the next car, or next level, and you'll be clear of the gap and so grateful that you had the faith and guts to keep moving forward.

Do Not Turn Back.

WORK THE EGO

Dissolving the Ego is a big waste of energy and time. You're not a monk. You have shit to do and you can't sit around all day meditating.

Instead you need to treat the Ego like a dog and put it to work. Without an assignment, a job that is big enough to keep it interested and entertained, it will wreck your life.

I had one client who wanted to downsize her life by moving into a house by the lake and not doing a particular Soul-draining kind of business anymore. She could plenty afford this scenario.

Yet, Egos don't care what you can and can't afford. They have a party line and that is: YOU CAN'T AFFORD THIS! Poor people have a hard time believing that Egos are assholes to well-off people about money, but they can be if they are left unchecked.

Anyway her Ego was all concerned about the numbers so we gave it a job to keep it busy.

First a little stroking: *Ego, you're so freaking amazing with numbers and budgets. I don't think we can possibly ever move to the lake. But if anyone can figure out how we can afford it it's you. Would you please do me a favor and call some real estate agents and make a Power Point presentation about how we can make this happen?*

Guess what? Her Ego got on board and felt important and found the way to make it happen. They built the house, saved money and she made even more money doing the type of work her Soul loves.

Put your Ego to work. Stroke it and give it an assignment. If it has concerns, tell it to solve them.

We don't have enough time?

Ego, please work out the calendar.

We don't have enough money?

Ego, please find a way to make some.

VISUALIZATION

My spiritual manifestation journey began with The Law of Attraction and I've been consumed with the study and experimentation of it for the last nine years or so. This spiritual reality saved my life after my darkest days post-9/11.

However, I didn't just follow it blindly. I kept records and wrote things down and did experiments with my friends and later with my masterminds and my clients. If it's a law, or a science, it should be replicable every time, so they say.

My results have been mixed, but I've witnessed so many miracles that I wholeheartedly believe that it works and I teach the methods to my clients, masterminders and anyone else who asks me for advice.

Here's a good example of what I mean by mixed results. I do a dream board every year. In fact, my whole family does and we have a big annual Dream Board party the first week of January. We've gotten enough results that we don't put something on the board unless we're very serious about getting it. Some of the time we get exactly what we asked for. Other times we get something that's just slightly "off."

For instance, I put my Dodge Grand Caravan on my dream board and went to the car place and told him what I wanted: red, clean, low miles, leather, all the bells and whistles for under $8,000. Oh, he laughed and laughed.

Three weeks later he called and said I would never believe it, but an older couple had just come in and said they bought this van thinking they would be driving their grandkids around but they haven't used it much and it has almost no miles and all the bells and whistles and they're willing to trade it in for $7,500.

My life is full of these stories. I'm a believer. I study other people's thoughts on it as well. Visualization is one way that most manifestation coaches will tout. Just visualize what you want so intensely that it's like you already have it. Visualize it over and over and over for twenty minutes a day. Jump around in your living room believing that you have it. Speak as if it is already so and then eventually it will be yours.

Good golly you can't imagine how much of my life I've spent trying to visualize stuff that I want. Sometimes I've gotten what I visualized so exactly it was eerie.

Sometimes I do not get what I want no matter how hard I try.

Sometimes I get what I want and then it feels nothing like I imagined it.

I started noticing that there were different qualities to the visualizations. If it is difficult to visualize, my results were less likely to be positive. I noticed that sometimes visualizations happen without conscious effort, they are things we catch ourselves daydreaming about. Other times I just can't keep the vision in my head. Still other times I would imagine the way something would feel and it would be amazing and then when I got it, it would be flat.

After my years of examination I began my Year of YES! experiment where I put the visualizing practices away and started to follow my Soul rather than try to attract something to me or make something happen.

Here's what I learned:

The visualizations that come so effortlessly that I catch myself daydreaming them are my Soul's longings.

The visualizations that I can't hold onto in my mind are not mine. They are some other thing in consciousness that I might be trying to want, but they do not belong to me.

The visualizations that I manifest but they feel flat when I get them are my Ego's desires or they are a least not my Soul's.

The things that haven't yet manifested are still coming.

TRACEE SIOUX

There are things happening right now in the Universe that we can't yet see.

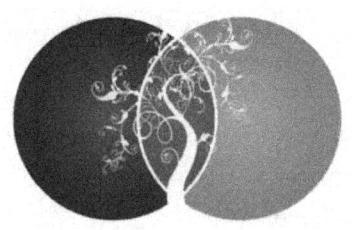

SOULFUL SERENDIPITY

In addition to annual dream boards, my spiritual manifestation practice includes choosing a word for the year. YES! was not my first word, but it was the one I wrote a memoir about. My word in 2015 was Serendipity because the year prior I had looked at my results and realized that the things that I had most enjoyed that year were the things I could never have thought to ask for.

In other words, my best gifts from the Universe that year were not the things I painstakingly cut out and pasted on my dream board, or the man that I conjured up with my list of qualities that I think would make up the perfect mate or the things I had spent my energy visualizing.

They were the people that I met who I never knew would make me happy and the bread crumbs that the Universe left for me so that I would follow my Soul to an unexpected venture.

TRACEE SIOUX

One example of serendipity I'm referring to happened at a Hay House conference. I knew that I was publishing *The Year of YES!* that year, but I hadn't decided how I wanted to do it, whether self-publishing or traditional publishing. I honestly wasn't thinking much about it because it was only March.

Waiting for a speaker to take the stage I look down at my hand and laughed because I had written, "*Tracee books,*" on my own hand. I had no conscious recollection of doing it, but there it was. I laughed at my own silliness. Later in the conference I looked down after a meditation and saw that I had written in my journal, "*I'm going to start a publishing company.*"

How cute.

Now, I had other ambitions for that year and had never had fantasies or visualized starting a publishing company. So I told a friend or two about these funny things and moved on with my business.

I was making all sorts of publishing decisions that year. I had published with traditional publishers as well as self-published a book in the past. Now I was investigating the publishing industry from a business perspective about how I wanted to put my Soul purpose book into the world. I was realizing that traditional publishing is a terrible business plan for most authors. Not only are you footing the bill for your own marketing and publicity but they own your copyright, take your creative liberty, it takes them years to get a book on the shelves and you never see a profit most of the time.

It was the time that was the real clincher for me, due to my very real vaginal pushing. There was no way this could continue for the years it would take for me to find an agent, then a publisher and finally to get the book on the shelves.

Self-publishing was also not the best option because while I was fine figuring out all the administrative stuff that has to be done it really bothered me that I had to give up third-party creditability and my ever-cherished childhood dream.

I set up a publishing company, Sioux Ink, hired expensive photographers, designers and editors to make the best book possible and I went to buy an ISBN. As I wrote Sioux Ink into the blank for publishing company on the ISBN site, it occurred to me that I had started a publishing company, just as my Soul told me I would back in March.

Cute story, huh?

That's not the end of the story.

By January a poet I know, Winston Hampton, ask me if I would publish his book of mystical love poetry, *Rumi Would Have Laughed*. So I put together a publishing package that offered everything I had previously wanted in a publisher: to keep my copyright and creative liberty, provide professional editing and design and offer me third-party credibility.

A few months later, Janna Phillips, a woman I've never even met asked me to publish her memoir, *Out of the Blue, A Psychic's Memoir*. She heard of me through a friend.

As I was working on both of these books there were moments when I was deep in flow, my Soul was playing with the light of these two healer's words and I felt as though I was doing God's holy work. I took Janna's simple, disorganized, but beautiful, third-person fiction book into an extremely powerful first person memoir that I am very proud to put my publishing imprint on.

This! This! This!

God! God! God!

I had moments where I could feel my Soul dancing for joy as I edited and reorganized and worked my word magic on these two Soul purpose books.

That, my friends, is the definition of Soulful Serendipity.

So yes, you can visualize things into existence.

You should absolutely ask for what you want.

You should definitely insist on what you need.

Still, the super juicy magic is so awesome that you haven't yet thought to imagine it.

SOUL vs. EGO SMACKDOWN

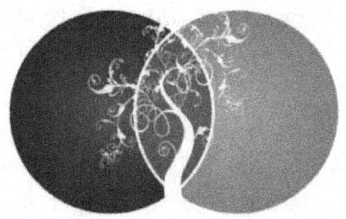

NOT 'TILL YOU'RE DEAD

The Outcome Isn't the Outcome Until You're Dead. Sweet, sweet Soul brothas and Soul sistas, can I make a very embarrassing confession?

I have lain on my floor in utter despair over my failure and defeat. I have cried. I have shouted, shaking my fists at the Universe, I have written scathing letters to God, I have gone to healers begging them to make my Soul to stop wanting hard stuff. I have stomped my feet and gone on Soul strikes. I have turned my back on writing (but only that once), I have hibernated in my house seeing no one, attempting to hide the shame of my failure. I have grieved deep and terrible grief and sighed deep and terrible sighs over my failure to live out whatever outcome I imagined that day.

The interesting thing is that you can faithfully push forward and achieve a huge milestone that your Soul has called you to do and even then your Ego will ruin it for you. That fucker.

The outcome isn't good enough. You have failed,
The Ego will taunt.

In reality what has happened is that you have been brave and courageous and faithful and strong and persistent and brilliant and you have produced a million megawatts of light for the planet through all of these amazing sparks you've created with this beautiful magnificent project.

But, no one cares.

No big check came.

One person criticized me.

Oprah still hasn't called yet.

Someone else did it better.

If you get hung up on the outcome this will be the internal dialogue:

Soul: I did it! It's so amazing! Look at the big light I just sparked!
Ego: You suck. Nothing you do matters.

The real jerky thing about this is that whatever the Ego is talking about is not the outcome. The outcome isn't the outcome until you are dead. Even then the outcome isn't the outcome.

People still stand in front of the Mona Lisa today, completely mystified by the everlasting light and mystery she contains. Even now, no one knows who she is.

SOUL vs. EGO SMACKDOWN

One spark.

Between painter and subject.

One spark between Leonardo da Vinci and viewer.

One spark between Mona Lisa and viewer.

Millions and millions of viewers long after both painter and subject are dead.

So don't let your Ego play that last dirty trick on you. He's knows you've made a huge leap forward and that you're not likely going back to your cave now, but that scares him so bad that he'll redouble his efforts and shame you and torture you with imaginary outcomes that haven't even happened yet.

TRACEE SIOUX

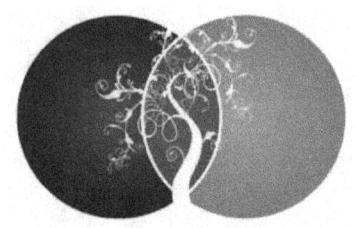

THINGS ARE HAPPENING

I was past a deadline for one of my clients on a big design project. I had bought a theme that had more bells and whistles but there was a learning curve that the designer and I were taking on. A lot of stuff was getting done on the project and we were nearing the finish, but I didn't have anything to show him yet.

Things are happening that you cannot yet see, I wrote him.

Then I realized that when I'm living my Soul's purpose things are happening that I cannot see all the time and that I shouldn't be so frustrated about what is or isn't manifesting right that second. Because it is manifesting, I just can't see every single nut and bolt move or every twist of the universal screwdriver.

Please remind me that things are happening that I cannot see the next time I get frustrated with the Universe, I wrote him.

Picture the entire Universe and everything you've asked for. Things are always happening that you can't see. Hanging on to that is what faith is.

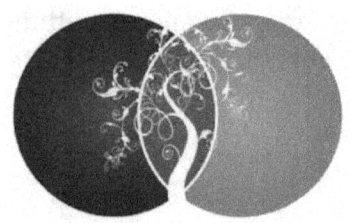

FEELINGS EARNED

Client: *I want to feel confident, I have such self-doubt and all these worthiness issues. I feel like other people have it so together and know that they can do what they want to do. I'm sick of feeing stressed out about money and I'm sick of my Ego telling me that this is my life and will always be my life! I want to have faith.*

Me: *You can't have what you want right now. I'm sorry to break it to you but there is no person out there who knows they can do everything they want to do. There is no person who feels unfailingly-worthy and never has self-doubt. There are only people who do it anyway. If you did not have faith you would not be going forward with your plan or sitting here with me. You've got the wrong idea about what faith feels or looks like. In the Bible everyone is talking about faith—but most of them are stranded in the desert on their knees yelling, 'God save me!'*

No, dear. The feelings you want to feel right now aren't yours yet. You get the confidence after you've done what you're trying to do. Not before.

SOUL vs. EGO SMACKDOWN

SOME FEELINGS YOU GOTTA EARN.

TRACEE SIOUX

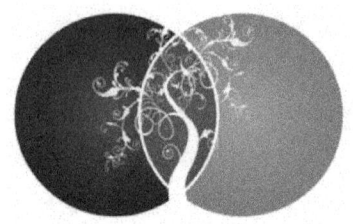

RED CARPETS

When you begin living this way the Universe rolls out the Red Carpet for you. But, it's a flying carpet and you have to leap off the cliff to land on it.

It takes a great deal of faith to say YES! to that still small voice that you can't name, see or touch. Especially because it is asking you to do things that your mother or your spouse might tell you are crazy. Even more so when it begins to threaten your Ego's safety by messing with your time, money and confidence.

Once you take the leap and land on the carpet there is enormous relief. Until it starts moving and you're not really quite sure where it's going to end up. Along the way—in the Gap—you'll end up in situations that you'll think you never signed up for and it's okay to curse when that happens.

I don't know where your Soul is going to take you. But I do know that the Universe begins working on your behalf in ways that will appear miraculous and magical because the Universe is interested in your Soul's expansion. Your Soul is interested in your happiness so the magic carpet ride should be a lot of fun if you can keep the Ego from freaking out.

Sometimes you will feel like you are winning.

Sometimes you will feel like you are failing.

Win. Fail.

Win. Fail.

But if you are trying at all, taking any step forward, you are winning. There are things happening in the Universe that you cannot yet see. I promise.

I do believe that you can have faith in this Soul promise:

Your Soul knows where it's going.

It knows the fastest and easiest way to get there,

And it will never, ever steer you wrong.

Say YES!

The Year of YES! MAXCELERATORS

Thank you so much for reading all the way to the end of this book. I'm so glad you honored me with your time and presence. I wrote this book with you in mind.

Someone who is calling for more.

More meaning. More purpose. More life. More time. More money. More happiness. More Love. More Light

I believe that living this way, following your Soul's guidance and learning to say YES! to it is the path to a deeper level of happiness and joy.

If you find that you'd like to continue on this path and need more support please join me over on Facebook: Tracee Sioux and Tracee Sioux: Law of Attraction Coach.

Please visit my website at www.TraceeSioux.com for more information, classes and resources.

ABOUT THE AUTHOR

Tracee Sioux is the creator, author and radio host of The Year of YES! Sioux did a one-year experiment where she said YES! to everything her Soul told her to do for one year. She now teaches others how to discover their own Soul's purpose and say YES! to it. Sioux lives in Colorado with her two children. Contact her at yes@traceesioux.com and visit www.traceesioux.com

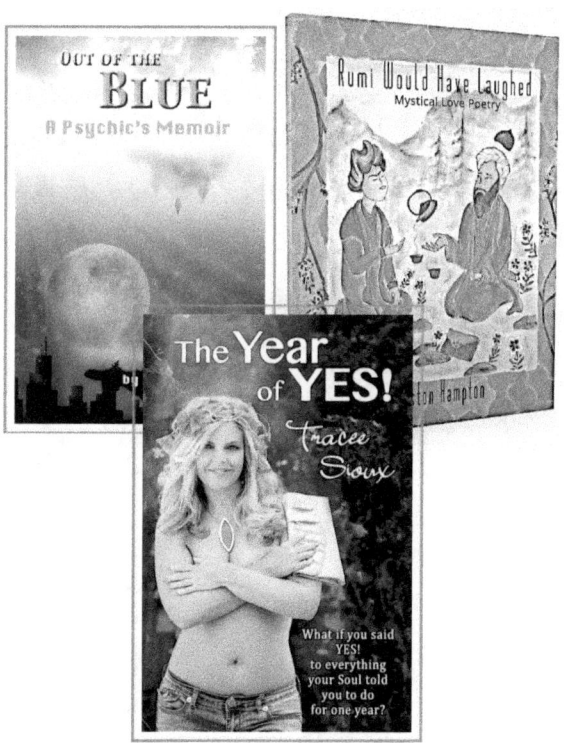

Sioux Ink Publishing Company is a full-service publishing company committed to assisting people publishing their Soul-driven books. If you have a book that your Soul insists that you birth into the world, please email yes@traceesioux.com.

www.ingramcontent.com/pod-product-compliance
Lightning Source LLC
Chambersburg PA
CBHW050534300426
44113CB00012B/2094